T0245987

Finding
Your Self at

The
Heartbreak
Hotel

Moving Beyond Betrayal

Finding
Your Self at

The
Heartbreak
Hotel

ALICE HADDON AND RUTH FIELD

HarperOne

An Imprint of HarperCollins*Publishers*

FINDING YOUR SELF AT THE HEARTBREAK HOTEL. Copyright © 2024 by Alice Haddon and Ruth Field. All rights reserved. Printed in the United States of America. No part of this book may be used or reproduced in any manner whatsoever without written permission except in the case of brief quotations embodied in critical articles and reviews. For information, address HarperCollins Publishers, 195 Broadway, New York, NY 10007.

HarperCollins books may be purchased for educational, business, or sales promotional use. For information, please email the Special Markets Department at SPsales@harpercollins.com.

FIRST EDITION

All notepaper art courtesy of Wasan Srisawat/Shutterstock, Elnur/ Shutterstock, Arthur Balitskii/Shutterstock, and Vovan/Shutterstock Art on pages iii, 1, 65, 133 courtesy of Katerina/stock.adobe.com

Photographs courtesy of the authors

Library of Congress Cataloging-in-Publication Data has been applied for.

ISBN 978-0-06-328995-6

23 24 25 26 27 LBC 5 4 3 2 1

To our mums
Tessa Haddon (1938–2020) and Kay Field

The Sun

She saw herself like a small creature
Laying in the sun, needing to keep warm to sustain herself.
And she moved with the light, never wanting to find
herself alone in darkness, shivering and cold.

She never realized… in the fog of her confusion,
in her concentration on keeping it all
together, in her fight to stay warm…

She never realized that even alone, she was never cold.

Because she was The Sun.
Radiant and burning from infinite reserves.
Nourishing small creatures and life for millennia
Powerful beyond all measure.

—ANI ALADEGBAMI

Contents

Contents

Part III: The Future

Devastation

You thought it was one way and it turned out to be another.

Heartbreak hits us so completely, almost violently. It is known and felt in an instant, as if we have been punched. Yet it takes a slow and painful journey of months, sometimes years, to restabilize ourselves and integrate the awful truth of it; the paralyzing tiredness that follows is testament to just how much our bodies take the blow. Heartbreak is not just emotional—it's physical, concrete, experienced by our bodies. In heartbreak, our bodies temporarily lose their structural and emotional stability and we become vulnerable to everything and everybody around us.

Heartbreak, betrayal, deception, perfidy, treachery,

duplicity, faithlessness, abandonment, infidelity:[1] these words represent a violation of safety and a shattering of the core belief central to intimate relationships—trust. Gone is your emotional security, your trust in the appearance of things, and the future as you imagined it. The one you trusted has done you great harm, sometimes irreparable harm, and it feels truly awful. It's like being shoved into the Large Hadron Collider and left there indefinitely, or being thrown overboard and while the waves crash around you and you're struggling to breathe, you look up to your loved one for help—only to realize they chucked you in.

And it's not just the intimate relationship that has been blown apart, but often the entire social and emotional ecosystem that surrounded it and to which you both belonged. The shared friends, the new family, the stories, the history, the favorite haunts—all gone as you find yourself adrift not just from the person you loved but from the network of people and places that glued you together.

Anger, rage, confusion, nausea, sleeplessness, anxiety, sadness, helplessness, dread—replaying and reliving what happened and fantasizing about both revenge and reconciliation leave the heartbroken utterly exhausted.

It's like being strapped to a knife thrower's wheel and kept there day after day, going round and round, sharp objects coming thick and fast. It's no wonder that a staggering 67 percent of betrayed partners meet the criteria for post-traumatic stress disorder.[2] There have been various attempts to describe this experience more precisely: post-traumatic embitterment disorder,[3] post-infidelity stress disorder,[4] moral injury.[5]

So grave and heinous is the sin of betrayal, the poet Dante reserved the most awful place in his vision of hell for those who committed it—the ninth and final circle. Next stop, Lucifer himself. In this terrible frozen wilderness, those who commit this "sin of the heart" are condemned never to feel the warmth of love again. Immersed up to their necks in ice for all time, they lie in grotesque positions, ears frozen off, eyes blinded by icy tears of despair, and with no prospect of reprieve.

Let's leave them there.

Betrayal most often comes to light in a sudden and catastrophic moment of discovery—a graphic sexual message on a phone, a bank statement revealing undisclosed trips, a text message sent to the wrong person by mistake. And only then do you see the lies that led up to it; only in retrospect is the web of deceit revealed. Most humans are surprisingly bad lie detectors (something that proficient manipulators exploit), and we tend only to spot their duplicity when it's right in front of our eyes.[6] And being duped feels both painful and humiliating. Added to this is another nasty feeling that lurks in the ashes of the betrayal–contamination. If you discover that your partner has had sex with someone else, you can be left feeling polluted, dirty, and contaminated. And much as an OCD sufferer washes their hands compulsively to rid themselves of germs, the betrayed get locked into an obsessive cycle of rumination in the hope it will rid them of the feelings of humiliation, violation, and degradation that accompany the betrayal.[7]

In terms of magnitudes of loss, there is much that heartbreak shares with grief, but with one central difference. Unlike the bereaved, the heartbroken must contend with the feeling of personal rejection, a feeling that cuts right to the place where we are most vulnerable, to the quiet voice inside us all that asks, "Am I lovable?" And the very person you would usually look to for reassurance is the one who has made you feel that you're not. Heartbreak relegates you to a place of the seemingly unwanted and unloved, and with it goes your power. Old hurts, sometimes stretching back to childhood, can rear their heads in times of rejection, further diminishing your sense of worth and self-esteem. Given this context, it's no wonder that you're spending heroic amounts of mental energy trying to rectify the situation and make it stop through ruminating on all manner of possible scenarios in an attempt to restore a sense of self-worth, punish your heartbreaker, or try to make them love you again.

Love is in fact such a powerful motivator that it has been likened to the rush of taking cocaine. Love releases a flood of dopamine, and the loss of it can leave the heartbroken behaving like drug addicts in search of their next fix.[8] You think you're done with them, but then they throw you a bone (or a crumb) and you're back where you started, grabbing the car keys and driving right over. And the hit is all the stronger if the crumbs are thrown intermittently. The fluctuating dopamine hits of early courtship—*Do they, or do they not love me?*—are mirrored in the torturous dynamic of heartbreak. One unexpected text message in the dead of night saying they miss you and the dopamine rushes in, compelling you to cling on.

Heartbreak has long been the subject of songs and novxiv   Introduction

els, but science has largely ignored it in favor of examining the process of falling in love. The lack of guidance from the psychological and scientific community has left the heartbroken to deal with a catastrophic experience of epic proportions with pat phrases like "There are plenty more fish in the sea," or "You'll find someone else," which are completely off-key. When you are betrayed and heartbroken, the last thing on your mind is getting back in the saddle or falling in love again, yet never in human history has it been easier to do just that.

The social revolution of internet dating has created a fast-paced, casual approach to romantic relationships. Take the dating site Ashley Madison[9]—whose tagline reads, "Life is short. Have an affair." It has an estimated membership of 75.90 million worldwide with nearly 400,000 new accounts opened every month,[10] indicating a mind-blowing amount of infidelity. There is some consensus that infidelity occurs in approximately one-quarter of all marriages and monogamous relationships,[11] and is the biggest predictor of relationship breakdown and divorce—ahead of lack of compatibility, falling out of love, addiction, and abuse.[12] And the fallout doesn't end there...

In 1990s Japan, doctors noticed anomalies in some patients who were presenting with heart attacks at emergency rooms but showing unexpected patterns of injury and recovery. Scans showed an odd shape to the heart, similar to the pots used to trap octopuses, which led to the condition being given the Japanese name takotsubo syndrome (*tako*–octopus; *tsubo*–pot).

Brought on by stressful and sudden events, such as hearing bad news, financial disaster, unexpected loss, a fierce argument, or even a surprise birthday party, takotsubo syndrome (a.k.a. broken heart syndrome) has no biological root cause. Its symptoms, however, are indistinguishable from a heart attack: chest pain, shortness of breath, and electrocardiogram abnormalities. Yet, beyond the octopus-pot shape-shift of the heart, there are no other physical signs or arterial obstructions, and unlike the more life-threatening cardiac arrest, recovery is usually quick.[13] Takotsubo syndrome has since been reported in almost every part of the world. Thousands of people are affected by it every year, and in the UK alone it makes up at least 7 percent of all heart attacks.[14] And 90 percent of those cases occur in women between the ages of fifty-eight and seventy-four.[15] Read that again.

In the West, the leading explanation for this is hormones (feeling hormonal again?). The depletion of estrogen during menopause is said to make women more susceptible to broken heart syndrome as their heart muscles have lost the natural protection against stress that estrogen provides. But if this were the whole picture, you'd expect boosting estrogen through hormone replacement therapy in menopausal women to solve the problem, but it doesn't.[16] Similarly, once women reach their midseventies and have the least amount of estrogen—if any—you'd anticipate rates to go up. But again, this is not the case.[17]

In South Korea, the term *haan* describes a feeling of unfairness and helplessness combined with a deep urge to right the wrongs of unresolved injustice. "*Haan*-ful" experiences can lead to what the South Koreans term *hwa-byung*—"fire disease." Clinically similar to takotsubo, but extending the scope of possible causation, *hwa-byung* is thought to be brought on by injustices and breaches of trust, including infidelity.[18] For the South Koreans, *hwa-byung* is about gender inequality and the suppression of women. Living within narrowly defined roles with little agency and influence over their lives, South Korean women find their anger piling up and up until their hearts give in.[19] Could it be that a lifetime of being in service to others has worn women out? That simply being a woman in this world is enough to break our hearts?

Researchers in Sweden have explored the link between life experience and broken heart syndrome and have included men in their study.[20] The interesting thing about their results is that the life experiences of men with broken heart syndrome map almost perfectly onto the women's. Both male and female participants spoke of being, "worn down to the bone" with never-ending demands and responsibilities, of being treated unjustly, of not having their own needs met, and all the while protecting, helping, and worrying about others without sufficient agency to change their situations. Hormones? Maybe. But what the Swedes have found points toward sociocultural frameworks of power. Far beyond the endocrine system lies the systemic betrayal of those with the least power by those wielding the most.

The truth is that women are still living against a backdrop of marginalization, disenfranchisement, objectification, and subjugation. Embedded within the ecosystems of our relationships, families, social groups, and cultures are deeply held values and beliefs. When it is revealed that shared values of equality and justice serve some and not others, we experience not just a personal betrayal but an ideological one. The tendrils of the dominant agenda reach right down into our souls, infusing us with messages that hurt and demean. When we are repeatedly told that we are not enough, that we are worth less, that we lack value, we start to believe it and these messages become internalized. And what's worse is we blame ourselves, as a psychological survival strategy to keep safe against those forces more powerful than us.

Women all over the world are coming alive to themselves and are fed up with being defined and treated in ways that are diminishing, invalidating, and harmful. The #MeToo movement showcased the mighty power of taking a stand together and made public what women have always known—that their lives are not a commodity and that their bodies are not for others.

When women are told it's all because of their hormones; when women are seen to be worthy of less respect and dignity than others; when domestic work done by women all over the world, imperative to their family's survival, is not valued through pay or status; when those in power make legal decisions about our bodies without consent or adequate consideration; when gender-based violence is tolerated; when women who bring charges of sexual misconduct, assault, or abuse are sued for defamation...

... it is a betrayal.

*   *   *

Ruth and I, a coach and a psychologist, have been friends since university, our conversations through the years often turning to our many heartbreaks: bereavement, betrayal, mental illness, rejection, loss of one kind or another, and more often than not finding something to laugh at in the face of terrible darkness.

Therapists aren't always that proficient at being vulnerable, although our business hinges on being able to help others navigate their vulnerability. In fact, it's not uncommon for therapists to enter the profession precisely to manage and even avoid their own fragility. Psychological understanding of the kind therapists digest helps create an illusion of structure and understanding around experience and an attendant sense of control. Yet, despite the comforting frameworks, experience and vulnerability always break through.

Just as being a doctor doesn't protect you from illness,

neither does being a psychologist protect you from pain. I too have succumbed to thoughts of *I should be over this by now,* and *No one wants to hear about this anymore.* I can't count how many times I've counseled against this kind of inner talk—holding the flag for loss and heartbreak needing time, and lots of it—and criticized the cultural and societal mores that tell all of us to "get back up on your feet."

We have both learned through personal and professional experience that when we are in pain we need care—intensive care—and that we also need space and time, connection, deep empathy, and kindness. This is what you need now too. To offer you that sense of safety and wraparound care, we've re-created the experience of being on retreat with us in these pages, as if you were a guest at the Heartbreak Hotel, searching for answers in the embers of your loss. Together with your fellow women guests—Nadia, Eshe, Lin, Irene, and Robyn, who you'll be meeting soon—we're going to discover what's next for you. Our wish for you, for them, and for all women is that you rise and shine. And we're going to show you how.

If you're finding it hard to stop scrolling through social media looking at the one they've chosen over you; if you're struggling to find a way to feel differently about your heartbreaker; if your friends have called time on listening to all the drama; if you've tried everything from sound baths to ice baths to hypnosis to drowning your sorrows in wine or sugar; if you take a few steps forward only to be thrown right back into the eye of the storm; if you're feeling as though your soul has been smashed into smithereens and left in pieces on the floor; if you feel helpless and exhausted and depleted and confused and angry and scared of being alone and have forgotten who you are outside of your shattered relationship; if you're railing against the unfairness and injustice and cannot make sense of it all and yet are determined to keep on trying...

...this book is for you.

PART I

The Present

CHAPTER 1

Welcome to the Heartbreak Hotel

We're glad you're here.

While you're with us, we'd like to invite you to take a break from your responsibilities and let us look after you for a while. What we do is gentle and powerful, and while you may feel a bit unsure, everything we do has a clear purpose—to get you back together with yourself. It may feel hard at times—we'll be asking you to be with your feelings of heartbreak and to try out new ways of dealing with them—but the act of faith that you are taking now, in being here and placing your trust in us, will be worth it. Take your time; don't hurry yourself. There is no rush.

We want you to feel cocooned in warmth and safety. Heartbreak can be traumatic, so we'd encourage you to wrap yourself up. Have a soft blanket nearby and cozy into it when you feel vulnerable. Create a sense of safety around you: light a candle, diffuse some essential oils, and limit any interruptions as best you can. Shortly you're going to meet your fellow women. They too have been heartbroken. You will hear echoes of your own experience in theirs, and while you may resonate with some more than others, remember that they are all trying their best in difficult circumstances, just like you. You may get upset as you hear their stories, and difficult feelings may surface; this is your empathy and compassion. You need it; we all do, because it is through sharing our vulnerabilities that we connect most deeply to each other and to ourselves.

You may feel exposed at times too, but we want you to know that we will never ask you to do anything we haven't done ourselves. It is through coming together in this way that we'll begin to reframe what's possible for you, and for all women. Stick with it. You are about to discover what happens when your individual experience is met by the power of the collective.

If you're thinking it all sounds a bit intense and that you're going to be sobbing your way through the experience, rest assured that for every tear shed there will be joy too. But we're not going to lie. You're going to go through a lot of tissues. But while painful things may come up for you, feelings are like bell curves: they peak and subside, and this is a pattern you will learn to trust as we go along.

Our retreats are alcohol- and technology-free, so we invite you to leave your phone in another room and refrain from the wine while you're with us. Both act as a distraction and have a numbing influence on your feelings; they are a way of avoiding those feelings, and avoidance ultimately prolongs suffering. While you're here, we want you to have a protected space where you can be with yourself and each other and where you're not going to be thrown off course by a bottle of wine or an unsettling message. So just for a while, turn off your phone and give the wine a miss so that you can stay with your feelings and not take yourself away from the knowledge and wisdom they contain.

Are you ready?

CHAPTER 2

Your Story

Before we go on, there is an important task we'd like to invite you to complete. The five women who will be joining you have been asked to do the same:

We would like you to write down the story of what has happened to you, the story of your heartbreak.

Writing down thoughts and feelings has long been used as an outlet and processing device for difficult experiences.[1] Getting it all out and onto the page will create some physical distance, so you can start looking *at* your story rather than seeing your experience from *inside* of it.[2] This will help you organize your thoughts and gain clarity over your feelings and experience, creating an opportunity for reevaluation. When you write your experience down in concrete and explicit terms, your relationship to your heartbreak can shift, positioning you as the narrator of your own experience. The trauma of heartbreak can leave your whole system adrenalized, and writing it down can help process your distress and calm your system.[3]

There is no expectation about how it is written; the length, style, and number of expletives are entirely up to you, and no one else ever needs to read it. We know this can feel hard—you may suddenly remember something vitally important you have to do right now instead! But remember, getting onto paper what is going round and round in your head is going to give you the control and distance from it that you need.

Imagine a glass of water with a layer of sunken mud at the bottom. Every time you touch the mud, it gets all stirred up and the water turns cloudy. So, you try to leave it alone and avoid it, but walking away just keeps you stuck in the muddy waters. If you want clear water in your glass, you need to get the mud out, and the only way to do this is to stir it up first and then filter it out. Writing down your story is the first step in your journey toward clarity.

If you're not ready to write your story yet, that's okay, you can wait a bit. And if you don't want to do it at all—

ever—that's okay too. But if you do, we invite you to frame it around the following questions:

What happened to you?

How has it affected you?

What sense have you made of it?

As you write, and indeed as you hear your fellow women's experiences, things may come up for you; this is natural and to be expected. But if you feel yourself becoming distressed or overwhelmed, we'd like to share with you a simple and effective way to help regulate your feelings...

Dropping Anchor

When dropping anchor, the first thing to do is to accept that the emotional storm is happening.[4] At the same time, expand your awareness of the present moment by noticing two or three things about your surroundings: the smell of clean laundry, the sound of rain on the roof, that the floor beneath your feet is hard or shiny.

Next, push the tips of your fingers together and press your feet into the ground. Take several deep slow breaths . . .

. . . and accept that the storm is happening.

Sometimes all we can do is drop anchor and hold fast until the storm has passed.

And pass it always does.

As you go through the book, "Dropping Anchor" is something you can hold in mind to create a sense of safety and to return to whenever you need. We'll indicate as we go along when we think it might be particularly helpful—we'll call them "Dropping Anchor" moments—but for now, while you're taking the time to write your story, you can have a go and practice.

As well as metaphors and regulation techniques like this one, we will also be introducing a few meditations along the way. When one is about to come up, we'll let you know, and we suggest that you read it through once or twice and then afterward close your eyes and try to faithfully complete the steps from memory. It doesn't matter if you need to do this a few times to get it right; read it through as many times as you like. After all, there is no rush.

You'll need a pen and paper or a journal; keep these handy while you read on. We invite you to specifically write by hand rather than typing as this will slow down your thoughts and give you more time to choose your words and connect with your feelings. We'd like you to dig out a photo of your younger self too, somewhere before the age of ten. You don't need to do this right away, but have a think where one might be and when it's a good time, retrieve it and pop it into your journal or keep it safe for later on.

Okay, let's meet your band of women now and hear what they've been going through.

CHAPTER 3

Scene I

Betrayed

NADIA   in her twenties, dark-brown hair cropped
        short, smooth brown skin, has an air of
        cool detachment. She's wearing a denim
        jumpsuit, and her hands often disappear
        into the black long-sleeved shirt she
        wears beneath it. She leans forward
        keenly, quietly inquisitive, waiting.

IRENE   a spritely seventy-one-year-old. She has
        short white hair and wears an oatmeal
        cardigan with comfy jeans. She is quick to
        laugh and tease. But there is a hesitancy
        about her, as if she's not sure whether she
        should be here.

ESHE   a senior lecturer in social sciences in her
        forties. She used to go by Stella, but since
        May 2022 has reverted to her birth name.
        Her wide-set eyes are framed by a mass of
        neat braids. She wears a loose cotton shirt
        and fiddles with the cross on her silver
        necklace.

ROBYN   in her sixties. She wears a brightly colored
        long dress and silver bangles that jangle
        on her tanned wrists. Her long silver hair
        is worn loose. She has a small unopened
        bottle of gin stashed in her laundry bag.
        She tells herself she won't drink it but

that she needs it near. She's thinking about
leaving, leaving and drinking.

LIN   in her late thirties, poised and contained,
         almost painfully polite. She sits up very
         straight, always close to the edge of her
         seat as if quietly striving to occupy the
         least amount of space. She's worried she
         won't fit in and seems uncomfortable in her
         clothes. She admires RUTH's green jumpsuit,
         even though RUTH tells LIN that her son
         said she looks like Shrek.

ALICE   in her late forties, wearing a loose blue
         dress. She has a quiet confidence and
         gentleness that puts everyone at ease.

RUTH   in her midforties, wearing a bright-green
         jumpsuit. To be fair, she does look a bit
         like Shrek. She is smiley and busy and keen
         to make sure everybody has what they need.

YOU   dear reader, yes, *you*. Please join us.

Cozy den. Evening.

A cozy den with two deep-blue velvet sofas facing
into a low coffee table. ALICE bends down to light
a large candle. A fire crackles in the hearth, an
armchair on either side. RUTH pours glasses of water
and sets them down, fluffing and plumping cushions
as she goes about the room. A low hum reverberates.
The sound of footsteps follows and the women enter
the room and settle themselves onto the sofas. RUTH
and ALICE sit in the armchairs on either side of the
fire, with NADIA to ALICE's left, followed by IRENE,
ESHE, ROBYN, LIN, and YOU. Each has brought their
story with them, and they all have a blanket at hand.

RUTH: [*Standing.*] Welcome, everybody. It's
         wonderful to have you here. Get comfy in
         your seats and let us know if there's
         anything you need. You may be feeling a
         bit anxious about your story, and that's
         okay-we're all a bit nervous. After all,
         we've only just met and we are about to
         do something quite exposing, so it's no
         wonder we're all feeling a little nervous.
         It was a big step for you all to write
         out your story, and now we're asking you
         to take another step and read it aloud to
         a group of almost strangers. We won't be
         strangers for much longer, that's for sure.
         So, before we ask each of you to read out
         your heartbreak story to the group, I'm
         going to set the intention for us all to

be compassionate and kind to one another
as we bear witness to each other's painful
journey, by reading aloud a loving-kindness
meditation, which we'll do together now.
Sound good? [*Smiles, looks to each woman.*]
Okay . . . here we go . . .

Take a moment to get settled and turn your
attention to the sensations of your heart. We don't
often take the time to check in with the state of
our heart. Is there tension there? Is there sadness?
Relief? Anxiety? Can you feel your heart? Just
take a moment to really notice what's there. Not
to think about it, but to feel it from the inside
out. While you do this, I'd like you to imagine
and hold in mind all the women around you who
have been heartbroken. Each one is a person who
experiences emotions, like you were just noticing
inside yourself. Each has been hurt, just like
you. Each of them has felt happy at times, just
like you. Each has been proud, just like you. Each
of these women has felt unworthy or inadequate,
just like you. Each of them wants to be happy and
content with their life, to feel that their life has
meaning, just like you. And each of them has found
it hard to achieve these things. Each suffers more
than they want to, just like you.

[*Pause.*]

See if you can connect with how hard it is to live
a human life. Being human is not easy. There may be
a sense of heartache or sadness as you contemplate
this situation that we all find ourselves in. Here
we are, each of us, faced with this situation of
how to live a human life. You are now going to
silently offer kind wishes to yourself and your
fellow women, and as you do, see if you can connect
with the sensations and feelings in your heart.

May we all be well.
May we all be joyful.
May we all be safe and at ease.
May we all accept ourselves as we are.
May we all be kind to ourselves.

[*Pause.*]

Can you feel right now, in this moment, that
you belong to something larger than your own
heartbreak? The next time you're in pain, please
practice remembering your wish for yourself and
your fellow women. Take a moment now to recognize
that you have just done something skillful and
kind, for yourself and for those around you.

It's time now for you to read your stories to each
other, and as each of you reads, the rest of us are
going to listen with our fullest attention, without

judgment or comment. Nadia? [*The women shift in their seats.*]

NADIA: [*Sips water, hands trembling; stands then sits.*] I didn't know how to write my story, so I just wrote answers to some of the questions you suggested. But it came out in a different order. Is that okay?

ALICE: However you've written it is exactly right.

NADIA: Okay, here goes . . . [*Clears throat, papers quivering.*] I met Aanya at a friend's wedding two years ago. I spotted her in the restroom trying to get a poppy seed out from between her teeth, and her lack of self-consciousness made me smile. Later at the bar when I was talking to a friend about how good the food was, Aanya was suddenly standing there telling us how the heat releases oils from the curry leaves, which intensifies the flavors, and I thought—Wow, she's smart. I soon discovered she was a lab chemist and obsessed with science; so different from me. I loved listening to her talk about it—amide bonds and oscilloscopes or whatever. And my God, did she love telling me about them. I took her number that night; thankfully the

attraction was mutual. I slotted into her
world fast. I'm good at that because
I never lived in one place for long as a
kid, and six months later we were living
together in her flat overlooking the river
Thames. Five months after that she asked
me to marry her. Of course I said yes! I
was infatuated. My mum ordered silks from
Assam for my dress and everyone was so
happy for me.

[*Pause.*]

Not long after our engagement, Aanya-writing her
name still makes me feel so sad-was offered a
promotion that meant going to Barcelona for six
months. I was happy for her and thought traveling
to see her would be fun-and it was, for a while.
But one day she called me from Spain and said she
couldn't go through with the wedding. It came from
out of nowhere. I was standing up when I took the
call, and I sank to the ground when she said that.
My knees just gave way. I felt winded, like the
life had been punched out of me. I remember gripping
the side of the table to steady myself-it was a
wedding gift from my auntie that had been delivered
that day and was still in its plastic cover-and I
remember despite everything that was happening being
distracted by the thought of having to return it

and explain why. When I finally found my voice,
it sounded unfamiliar, as though it belonged to
someone else. I was shaking, shivering, and talking
really fast, but I cannot remember much of what
I said. My mouth was completely dry. She sounded
cold and distant; I didn't recognize her at all. I
couldn't understand why she was doing this . . .
but she didn't want to talk about it; the call was
short, her goodbye so abrupt . . .

[*Pause.*]

Then the texting began. I asked her what had
happened, implored her to come home, told her she
was crazy to throw it all away, pleaded with her
to just pick up the phone. I said we'd be okay once
we were together again. I was determined that if I
carried on as normal, then it wouldn't really be
happening. She didn't reply to any of my messages.

[*Pause.*]

I talked to my cousins and friends-one even offered
to call and talk to Aanya-but in the end, there
was no need. She flew back a week later, and the
second she set foot inside our flat she told me
she'd met someone else. I asked her if she loved her
and she said yes, she thought so. I asked her if
she'd slept with her and she said she had. I asked

her if she still loved me and she said she thought
she did, but that she felt trapped. She didn't
try to comfort me, even though I was crying and
begging her to give us another chance. No matter
what question I asked, her answer was the same:
it's over. She said it so many times. At one point
I fell to my knees, and was holding on to her
leg, begging her to reconsider, but she flinched
and shook me off like a dog. [*Lip quivers, teary
cheeks;* LIN *passes her tissues.*]

[*Pause.*]

I can't move on. I keep having the same
conversation over and over again with my family and
friends and anyone at work who'll listen, and I
never get any clearer about anything. They all say
if she treated me like that, I'm better off without
her, but I just get more upset. I knew she was
single-minded and sometimes selfish, but I'd always
seen this as a good thing. I loved her for it. I
just can't believe she dumped me and has left me
with all these unanswered questions, which leaves me
feeling hollowed out. I'm struggling to concentrate
at work too, because all I can think about is the
other woman. I've since discovered she's a colleague
of Aanya's and beautiful in a way that I know I'm
not. I can't stop scrolling through her social
media; it kills me, but I keep on doing it. I can't

sleep. I have nightmares about killing them both,
then wake up in a cold sweat and my heart breaks
all over again when I realize they are both alive-
and probably in bed together. [*Laughs through
tears, retreats to the back of the sofa, draws
up her knees;* RUTH *wraps a blanket around her; a
moment's silence as everyone takes it all in;* ALICE
nods to IRENE.]

IRENE: Oh right, me now. Gulp. Okay . . . Two
       years after my husband, Stan, died, my
       friend Claire persuaded me to join a dating
       website. It was a week before my seventieth
       birthday when she came over to help set
       up my profile. It was a dating site
       specifically for widows and widowers, which
       in hindsight makes what he did to me even
       more upsetting. Claire and I had a rum and
       Coke, which helped me loosen up a bit, and
       I even dug out a red lipstick I'd not worn
       since I was a student nurse in my twenties.
       We were giggling like a pair of teenagers. I
       was three rum and Cokes down by the time she
       left, but I do remember admiring my red lips
       in the mirror and wondering why I'd never
       worn that lipstick when I was with Stan.
       I thought it strange I'd kept it for over
       forty years, and how vivid it was, despite
       all that time passing. I didn't think

anything of the dating site after that-I
had mainly done it to please Claire, and
it was only when I saw her a week later and
she asked me if I'd heard anything that I
thought of it again. Soon after that I got
my first message from Daniel. We hit it off
immediately. He asked so many questions-I
don't remember ever being asked so many-I
was flattered by his interest. I opened up
to him, about things I'd never even told my
husband. Now I just feel like I've betrayed
Stan's memory.

[*Pause.*]

Daniel called me "Reeny," and each time he did
that, my heart leapt. When we spoke on FaceTime,
I'd put on the red lipstick, like a silly teenager.
He told me he was working on a rig off Scotland,
which Claire checked out to make sure it was the
real deal. After a few weeks of talking every day
and many messages, he told me his brother had been
in a bad accident on the rig and broken both his
legs. He said the situation was desperate and that
his brother didn't have any money, so I offered
to help. Turned out he needed twenty thousand
pounds, which Daniel said he'd pay back as soon
as he'd been paid. He even sent me a picture of an
"invoice," which he said was due to be paid soon,

along with a photo of his brother's legs, all
mashed up.

[*Pause.*]

When I told Claire, she started on me with
questions: When were we going to meet up? Why does
he keep saying he can't get away? She said they
usually have long periods off from the rig, so
where was he? I asked Daniel myself, because I
was dying to meet him, and that's when he told
me he was coming to visit in three days. I was
so excited. I bought a new outfit and went to the
butcher in town to buy haggis-no idea how to cook
it, but he'd mentioned he liked it. I couldn't
eat a thing in the lead-up; I was pacing up and
down, in and out of rooms, rearranging chairs
and putting my lipstick on and then taking it
off again. I'm so embarrassed now that I could
have been so stupid, like a schoolgirl with a
silly crush. [*Hand on her chest, looking up for
reassurance; the women nod.*] But when the doorbell
rang and I opened the front door, everything was
okay. He was tall, rugged, and handsome, with a big
smile and neat white teeth. The opposite of my Stan,
who was ever so stocky and never had much hair.
He gave me a huge bear hug and made me feel at ease
right away. It felt so good to have him there after
so long being on my own. But I feel like such an

idiot now because there were signs. I see them
now in neon lights, but not back then. He was
always checking his phone, distracted by what
kept pinging up.

[*Pause.*]

He said it was his brother, but now I know he was
having conversations with other women-I don't know
how many. In the end, he could only stay the one
night, which at the time I thought was romantic as
he had traveled overnight from Scotland to get to
me. Now I'm wondering if he was ever in Scotland at
all. The next morning while we were drinking tea in
bed, he started up on his phone again and quickly
became upset. More trouble with his brother, who
needed money for another round of surgery. I was
still so happy from the night before and would
have given him the house if he'd asked for it. When
I saw the tears in his eyes, what could I do? Of
course I offered to help out. Just before he left,
he gave me clear instructions about what to say to
the bank when I asked to transfer the money-that it
was for renovations on my house so they wouldn't
question another large sum. I did exactly as he
instructed. But the bank wouldn't do it and kept
probing, so I ended up telling them the truth.

[*Pause.*]

I called Daniel to let him know what had happened.
He got tetchy at first and asked me to repeat
exactly what I'd told the bank. I said I couldn't
see the harm in being open about his brother,
feeling sure they'd understand. He changed then,
got so angry and started shouting at me, called me
a stupid bitch. I've never had anyone say that to
me my whole life. I was stunned, shaking all over,
and then I started to cry. He hung up. I didn't
know what to do. I was so upset and confused.
I'm ashamed to say that I crawled into bed and
cried myself to sleep, hoping I'd never wake up.
The police got in touch a few days later to ask
questions, and they told me they'd uncovered a
scam. Turned out Daniel was a fake and part of a
much larger criminal operation. I saw red then,
threw that bloody lipstick at the wall. I called
him so many times demanding an explanation, but
he'd disappeared off the face of the earth. Of
course he bloody had.

In the end I had to tell my daughter. I tried to
keep it from her, but she could tell something was
up. She's the one who found out about this retreat
and thought it would do me good. She's so kind to
me, sometimes I wonder if I deserve it. My sons are
in their thirties and forties and living their own
lives, and I don't have the heart to tell them. They
will think I've been so stupid. And I have. I never

should have trusted him. I wanted to spend some
time in Australia, visiting my sons and getting to
know my grandchildren better. I even entertained the
idea of Daniel coming along with me. What a bloody
fool I am. I can't believe I'm more heartbroken by
a man I only met once and knew online for just a
few short months than I was when dear Stan died.
I'm sorry. [*Looks up, then buries face in hands,
weeping; room falls silent; ALL look to* IRENE;
ALICE *turns to* ESHE.]

ESHE: [*Clears throat, plays with silver cross on
          her necklace.*] This is so hard . . . We
          met online and arranged to meet in a local
          bar; looking back, I see those two things
          held clues to the sort of man he really
          is. But I was inexperienced and shy, and
          at thirty-five years old, felt I needed
          to get on with it. He was intoxicating
          and I couldn't believe the purity of our
          connection. It felt so good; it felt right.
          He was generous in those early days, but
          it turns out he didn't have much money
          and what little he did have he never held
          on to for very long. After a while he
          stopped offering to pay for things, always
          claiming he was owed money by an unreliable
          friend. It didn't matter—they were only
          small things, like cinema tickets or ribs

at his favorite diner. At the time I paid
no attention to the fact that none of his
friends ever materialized. It was just him
and me in a bubble that nothing could pop.
I was so happy when he came to my church
and met the pastor, and six weeks after our
first meeting, he got down on one knee and
proposed in front of everyone at the diner.
I thought I might die of happiness when he
asked, but how quickly it all turned bad.
We married within six months, and I fell
pregnant almost straight away, and that's
when the cracks started to show. He started
staying out late and stopped paying money
into our joint account. He lied about his
work too, saying he was on a long shift
when he was at the bar. He drives a taxi,
so it wasn't always obvious. When he did
come home though, he was always on at me
either to do more around the house or to
improve my job situation and bring in
more money. When I was pregnant with our
second child, a head of department role
came up. I didn't think I could manage the
position, so I told him I wasn't going to
apply for it, and he was so unsupportive.
Even though he often came home late and
seemed disinterested in me, I longed for
his loving touch. I did everything I could

to try to bring back that warmth, but he
left me out in the cold. He was so loving
with the children, would laugh and play
with them, but switched mood the second I
tried to join in. We still had sex, but
it became transactional and only ever on
his terms. I often wept afterward, shocked
that this intimate, beautiful act that
had brought us so close together in the
beginning could have become so empty. He has
this swagger about him and liked to let me
know that others were interested and that
he could have had anyone, and I believed
him. I panicked I'd lose him. I kept
thinking I must have caused this change in
him; that it was all my fault. That there
must be something wrong with me that made
him treat me this way. That maybe I was
being punished for a crime I had forgotten
I'd committed-and I pleaded with God for
mercy . . .

[Pause.]

Straight after the birth of our third child, my
father died, and I remember my grief was tinged
with this intense anxiety about flying back to
Johannesburg and leaving him with the other two
children, fearful that someone would steal him

away from me while I was gone. It was soon after
I got back that his phone buzzed while he was in
the kitchen; I don't know why I looked, but I did,
and then I just couldn't stop. There were all these
graphic sexual messages from women with names like
Kitten and Cupcake. When he walked back in moments
later, I looked up at him in disbelief. He told
me of his terrible loneliness, that he didn't feel
important, and that I'd made him feel small, so
he'd sought comfort online-but that was all it had
been: online chat sites. He was so vulnerable then,
almost like a child, and I felt sorry for him. I
forgave him. I held him in my arms and comforted
him while he wept, all the time praying that the
children would sleep through it. He promised to
get help-and that night we made love and his tender
touch returned. I was full of hope that things
would get better. He said he went to see the pastor
to confess and promised to see a counselor, but
he never went, instead using the money I gave him
for the sessions to take drugs and have sex in his
taxi-and then he gave me an STD. The shame I felt
going to the clinic and realizing it must have been
from him . . . something broke in me that day. Rage
rose in me, and I chucked all his belongings out of
the house and threatened to tell everyone.

[Pause.]

He has since been back many, many times begging
forgiveness. Sometimes he cries. Sometimes he brings
me something. Last time he came with a small bunch
of yellow freesias that reminded me of home, but
they smelled sour, like altar wine gone bad, and I
threw them out. I am tearful and panicky all the
time. I feel like a tent whose middle pole has been
snapped in half, and everything is flailing around
me untethered. I am left picking up the pieces
of our lives and caring for three children while
working full-time. The worst part is that I still
love him, which makes me feel confused and pathetic.
How can I love such a man? But the children need
their father, and I can't do this on my own.
[*Folds up story, places it in journal, looks up,*
nods shyly, composing herself; after a pause ALICE
nods to ROBYN.]

ROBYN: I was diagnosed with multiple sclerosis
        early last year, and within two months, my
        husband of twenty-eight years announced he
        was leaving me because I was "boring and
        crippled." To begin with, I thought it was
        some kind of sick joke-he could be a bit
        like that. But when I realized he was being
        serious, my next thought was that he'd met
        someone. When I asked him, he swore blind
        that he hadn't, and I believed him-I still
        believe him. I never worried he'd stray
        because he's never shown any interest in

other women. I've never seen him so much as
flirt with someone else; he's too shy for
any of that. He told me he wanted to leave
because he believes there is a more "soulful
love" out there for him, and for me, and
I still don't know what the hell that's
supposed to mean.

[*Pause.*]

Our daughters don't know yet; they are both away at
university just now and he wants me to tell them.
What a coward. I know it will break their hearts
and I'm scared that they'll blame me. He should
damn well tell them himself. It makes me so mad. I
had thought we were a normal, averagely exhausted,
happy enough family, but apparently, he was not
thinking the same way and was not happy at all.
He now says that he never felt close to me, that we
never had a deep connection. He told me that I was
no fun and made him miserable, but that's just not
true! I'm not sure of anything anymore. By the way,
all these precious insights are coming to me via
text message from France, where he is camping out
in the house we've spent the last decade renovating-
our retirement project. He's probably installing
the mosaic bathroom tiles we found on a trip to
Santorini-I hate them now. Anyway, to say I am
heartbroken would be an understatement. The horror
of it all just keeps coming over me in waves. I

thought we were okay. Our sex life wasn't great,
I'll admit that. But I was wiped out a lot and
going through menopause, so I put it down to that.
Plus, he'd never had much of a sex drive himself,
so it didn't occur to me that this was a big deal.
It feels as though at the first hint of sickness,
everything we'd built together came tumbling down.
I am slowly realizing that I have been the only
adult in our marriage. I had three children to look
after, one of them being my husband.

[*Pause.*]

He is intent on a divorce, but he wants me to
organize it all for him! I am left alone in the
house we shared for more than thirty years. Our
marriage is everywhere and all around me. I am
afraid of the financial implications of all this
for my future, but more than that I'm terrified
of being alone. I am too old to start again, and
I have no idea who I am anymore. I cannot make
sense of it. I've been going through old photo
albums searching for clues to explain his sudden
disappearance. We weren't miserable; we barely even
argued. I can only think that since his work has
slowed down and he's spent more time at home that
he's having some sort of crisis. I'm devastated
that it's come to this. That's it. [*Looks up, then
casts eyes down.*]

[*Pause.*]

LIN: [*Twiddles strands of hair between fingers;
         eyes flit between ALICE and RUTH.*] Okay,
         here goes . . . Every time I put my key into
         the lock, I hold my breath. Sometimes, it's
         silent inside and I'll call out his name
         to check if he's there. Often he doesn't
         answer, so I assume he's out, but then I
         find him lying in the bath, which makes me
         jump, and then he sneers at me for getting
         spooked. Or he'll be lying on the bed fully
         clothed with his arms across his chest,
         staring at the ceiling waiting to catch me
         out. I am very careful about what I say to
         him on these occasions, if anything. But
         when I open the door to the smell of his
         delicious cooking, I'll feel hopeful again.
         This is now so infrequent that I'm starting
         to wonder if it ever actually happened.
         It's got to the point where the smallest
         thing can set him off, like not hanging my
         keys on the correct hook. I never thought
         I'd miss the days when he was sulking in
         the bath or lying on the bed, but I do
         sometimes. Anything is better than his
         contempt.

[*Pause.*]

It wasn't always like this. In the beginning, we
were happily exhausted medics working in different
parts of the hospital. I was a junior house officer
in radiology up on the third floor, and he was a
consultant anesthesiologist in the intensive care
unit raising people from the dead-that's how my
mother put it. I still fantasize about those early
days when he couldn't keep his eyes off me. We were
never apart; we'd spend hours wandering through the
botanical gardens holding hands and talking. I
loved how he looked after himself and treasured all
his belongings. Perhaps I should have thought that
was odd, but at the time I thought it was a sign
of his good character-that he took such good care
of them might mean he'd take good care of me.

[Pause.]

We used to mark off our shifts on the kitchen
calendar and coordinate our days off so we could
spend them together. But not anymore. Everything
changed when he moved hospitals last year. He became
possessive of my time and suspicious of what I was
doing with it, and if I ran over my shift, he'd
quiz me at length and always find fault with my
answers. I dreaded my pager sounding with last-
minute emergencies, afraid of provoking him, but
all I have to cling to now is my work, and I am
so grateful for it. On the nights when he isn't at
home, I've trained myself to enjoy the fact that

I have the place to myself and can leave my keys
wherever I want.

[*Pause.*]

When I'm at my most exhausted, he plays music to
torment me or sings loudly in the shower just as
I'm going to sleep. And whenever we are off work at
the same time, he leaves the apartment, overnight
bag in hand, almost the minute I'm home, no
goodbye and no telling me where he's going. I know
he doesn't visit his parents or sister. I have no
idea where he goes or who he is with. He doesn't
answer his phone or respond to my text messages,
so I've stopped sending them. When I get home and
he's back from one of these outings, I'll find him
asleep smelling of someone else. He likes to keep
me guessing; he enjoys baiting me. But if I dare
to question him too much, he flies off the handle.
When I get upset, he shouts that I'm imagining
things, that I've made it all up, that I am a
nightmare to live with. The rest of the time there
is this deafening silence, the atmosphere so harsh
and devastating, I feel like I could die. I found
a scarf that didn't belong to me and confronted
him about it. He flung it in my face and said I
was talking rubbish, that it was the scarf he'd
bought me last Christmas. He had bought me a scarf,
but it was not bright pink or made of silk like
this one. He sounded so sure about it and was so

angry at me for accusing him, that in the moment
I thought he might be right and perhaps I had made
a mistake. Two weeks ago, I tried to tell him I
wanted him to leave my apartment, but he laughed
in my face and told me he wasn't going anywhere.
He said nobody else would ever want me, that I'd
be on my own forever. I was stunned that he could
just dismiss me like that and carry on scrolling
through his phone as if I hadn't said anything
at all. I felt worth less than nothing to him.
[Pauses, takes a few deep breaths, looks up, smiles
at ALL.] I was desperate and had no one to turn
to, so I plucked up the courage to call my mother.
I'd barely got going when she told me how lucky I
am to have attracted the attention of a consultant
anesthesiologist and that whatever sins he has
committed I must forgive. I should have known
better than to hope for anything from her. [Voice
trails off.] I hate myself for being so weak.
[Raises eyes, tears fall.]

ALICE: Reader, are you ready to share your story
        with us?

[ALICE invites the group to check in with how they
are feeling in their bodies and encourages them to
bring to mind dropping anchor if they need to.]

CHAPTER 4

Rumination

The Trap

*D*id they use sex toys? Which ones? Did they use one of these? Tap, tap, tap. How long ago? Did they watch porn together? What kind? How recently? Did she tell her about me? When? Where? How? Is that another lie? Are they together now? Scroll, scroll, scroll. Instagram, WhatsApp, Facebook, head on fire, pulse racing, burn, burn, burn. Hold head, squeeze eyes, rock, rock, rock. How could she? Why, why, why? I don't understand. I'm going to be sick, I'm going to be sick, flick, flick, flick.

Nadia went over and over again in her mind what might be on her fiancée's phone. She imagined into existence all sorts of unspeakable sexual acts, endless mental images of her fiancée and her lover together, causing her acute pain. It was a compulsion, a form of self-harm she felt powerless to stop.

She spent many evenings with her cousin after she discovered her fiancée's infidelity. They'd drink wine late into the night, poring over texts and photos. Nadia would tell her cousin again and again about the awfulness and injustice of it all. Her cousin listened, wondering if it even mattered to Nadia that she was there—because it wasn't a conversation; it was Nadia's internal dialogue externalized, her attempt to get clarity on an unbearable situation that made no sense. It was an attempt to try to reach some kind of resolution so she could move forward. And she was angry. Very, very angry. Stuck in an endless loop of questions, desperate for answers that never came, Nadia was in terrible pain and her cousin felt helpless. Any attempt to encourage Nadia to stay with one point and examine it would be quickly swatted away. She didn't want to hear it. So, on and on she went. Round and round and round. And in the dead of night her quest for answers would take on a quieter and more troubling undertone that whispered, *There's something wrong with you.*

The foundations of rumination go deep, beyond the event itself to the very heart of our sense of self and the world around us. The existential imperative to understand our world and our lives is cloaked with another human need—to feel loved.

Nadia needed her anger and her quest for answers because it kept her from the painful feeling of no longer being loved. Her rumination seemed to be the only power she had left, the only control she could exert over her free fall. And in fact, there *was* a purpose to Nadia's rumination. It was a necessary protection her mind and body generated to shield her from the unbearable loss, bewilderment, and rejection that lay beneath her frenetic search for resolution.

Heartbreak creates an unbearable dissonance, a catastrophic split between how we thought things were and how they now appear to be. And the rumination is an attempt to restore equilibrium and create consonance once again. As meaning-making beings, we like to create organized frameworks and systems to inhabit in order to feel safe. If how we previously understood relationships conflicts with where we now find ourselves, we become intensely confused and anxious—it makes no sense.[1] Under the extreme distress and anger of rejection, our meaning-making machinery goes into overdrive, trying desperately to restore alignment.

Rumination is natural and inevitable in the aftermath of betrayal. It's a symptom of your intelligence that you do it. You are trying to figure things out and gain a sense of control, to reconcile what has happened, and make meaning from the wreckage. You are trying to put it all back together somehow, to repair it and to feel hopeful again. But then you can't sleep for thinking how it all came to pass, why it happened, how you didn't deserve it, and how alone and tired you are...how unjust the world is. So you try to think even harder to put it all to rights, and the vicious loop continues.

And the body takes the blow too. The headaches, accelerating heart rate, shaking, and nausea are all indicative of a body in high tension and stress. It's in the sleeplessness and frantic worry, the lack of concentration, the poleaxing exhaustion as you rip along at breakneck speed on the rumination roller coaster you never wanted to board but somehow now cannot get off. Rumination taunts and torments you like a jailer, keeping you awake and threatening you with a life sentence, while the person who has the answers is either long gone or disinterested in your need for them. It's torturous.

Your mind focuses in on the hostile event and gets stuck like an old record, repeating the same cycle, rarely giving you a conclusive or satisfactory answer ... and it's a costly business. It's like a repeated withdrawal of funds from your emotional tank, and before you know it, you're all out, in the red and being charged interest for the overdraft.

So powerful is it, that the rumination is almost impossible to contain and ends up spilling out into all your conversations and relationships. The heartbroken frequently enlist the help of friends to go over their betrayal in increasingly indignant circles of "co-rumination."[2] And the bigger the badder; as more and more friends are unwittingly enlisted into the rumination, it becomes a collective project. Yet this collective rumination, far from alleviating the pain, actually intensifies and accentuates your suffering by keeping you locked into the endless quest.[3] "Collective rumination," as it's known, can maintain anger not just for months or years, but through generations.[4]

As well as fueling your anger and increasing the stress in your body, rumination can reduce self-control.[5] In a ruminative frame of mind, you're left vulnerable to actions that you might later regret. Ever pressed send on a vitriolic text message you immediately wished you could retrieve? Driven over to your heartbreaker's house and banged on the door? Followed their new lover online or in person? Taken up smoking? Drunk excessive amounts of alcohol? Far from giving you control, rumination and its attendant stress can actually disable the stop button. And you can't just tell yourself to stop. What you resist persists, and telling yourself to stop only serves to keep the thoughts coming—often faster and more intensely. If we were to ask you *not* to think about a pink elephant for the next minute, could you do it? Have a go. It's a frustrating paradox: you can't tell your rumination to stop because that only intensifies it, and yet it's only when your rumination stops that you can get out of the cycle and move forward.

There is another way...

Letting go is the act of deciding not to struggle anymore with what has happened. It's not letting go of a person; your heart and mind will forever be populated by the people you have loved, even the ones who have hurt you. It is letting go of the struggle—day after day.

The Tiger Cub

Imagine you wake up one morning and just outside your front door is an adorable tiger kitten, meowing.[6] Of course, you bring the cuddly little thing inside to keep it as a pet. After playing with him for a while, you notice he is still meowing, nonstop, and you realize he must be hungry. You feed him a bit of minced meat, knowing that's what tigers like to eat. You do this every day, and every day your pet tiger grows a bit bigger. Over the course of two years, your tiger's daily meals change from hamburger scraps to prime rib to entire sides of beef. Soon your little pet no longer meows when hungry. Instead, he growls ferociously at you whenever he thinks it is mealtime. Your cute little pet has turned into an uncontrollable savage beast that will tear you apart if he doesn't get what he wants.

Every time you feed him, you help your tiger grow a little bit larger and a little bit stronger. Feeding him in this manner seems like the prudent thing to do; either you feed him whatever he wants, or he will eat you up. Yet every time you feed him, you enable the tiger to grow stronger and more intimidating . . . until the tiger controls you.

Your pain is the tiger, and your rumination is the food. The solution that rumination promised to be turns out to be the problem—now on steroids—that it was supposed to solve.

The Chinese Finger Trap

The struggle won't set you free.[7] When you are trapped in an experience, feeling as though you're drowning and being swallowed up by it, your instinct is to try to escape. Everything in you screams, "Get out! Find a way out! I can't bear it! Struggle more! Pull harder!" This is a completely natural survival strategy, and a useful one at times because it's your instinct talking. But there are some situations you can't escape in this way. Sometimes, struggling creates more of a noose than the rope itself. Think of quicksand, where the frantic movements of your body shift the sand so it sucks you further under. The way out—counterintuitive though it may seem—is to stay still, spread your body out, and float on the sand until it releases its grip so you can call for help or roll over to safety. We don't recommend you experiment with quicksand, but we do have something else to help you absorb the idea in a less gritty way—the Chinese finger trap.

This is a woven bamboo tube, not more than a few inches long, just wide enough for you to fit your index fingers inside. But once you've placed them inside, if you try to pull them out again, the weave of the bamboo constricts and the grip on your fingers tightens. The harder you struggle to get them out, the tighter the grip becomes. Maintain the force of the pull and you stay right where you are, trapped. If, on the other hand, you relax your pull and let your fingers just exist inside the trap with no tension at all, the weave of the bamboo slackens and expands, and you find there is ample room to remove your fingers and make good your escape.

The more you try to think your way out of the pain, the tighter the grip it has on you. Nothing is going to take the pain away, and we know it hurts like hell, but noticing when you're back in the struggle again, and choosing instead to let go, is how you'll begin to reframe your relationship to it. So, try to remember the Chinese finger trap—buy one if you like!—and use it as a reminder of how to let go.

CHAPTER 5

Scene II

Give Your Ex the Finger

Cozy den. Later that evening.

Fire crackles, footsteps sound, and the women reenter
the room and settle themselves back down. NADIA wraps
a blanket around her shoulders, sinking back into
the sofa corner. IRENE sits at the other end, placing
a folded square of blanket on her lap and patting it
down. ROBYN is on the opposite sofa, facing IRENE
and sipping water. LIN sits close to the edge of the
sofa and shivers. ESHE moves to LIN, takes a blanket
from the sofa arm, drapes it around LIN, and gives
her shoulders a squeeze before settling into her own
seat. ESHE sits cross-legged, leans in, fiddling
with her necklace.

RUTH: We're going to have some fun now and do a
         short exercise together.[1] It's lighthearted,
         but the purpose is deep-to reduce the power
         of your heartbreaker and all the nasty
         things they've said to you. We're going to
         do this by externalizing and then diffusing
         those criticisms, so they no longer feel
         as though they are part of who you are.
         Are you ready? Let the diffusion begin!
         So, first of all I want you to picture
         your heartbreaker: really see them in your
         mind's eye. I want you to imagine a time
         when they were really critical and harsh. It
         might be an isolated incident, it might be
         a barrage of criticism-it doesn't matter,
         just bring it to mind and really hear them
         saying those nasty things to you. Now

- 48 -

I want you to tune in to their tone of
voice while they're saying it-is it loud,
harsh, shouty? Really hear it. Have you
got it? Okay. Now I want you to change
the voice and make it really high-pitched
and squeaky, like a cartoon character,
and have them say the mean things in this
new silly voice instead. Have you got it?
Okay, great . . . Now extend your forearm
straight in front of you as far as it
will go, palm upturned. It doesn't matter
which arm you use, whichever feels most
comfortable. Curl up your fingers into your
palm and make a fist. Now raise the middle
finger. Okay . . . take the image in your
mind of your heartbreaker and transport
this image out from your mind and float it
all the way down your arm and onto the tip
of your middle finger, and as you do so,
shrink them down to the size of a thimble
so they fit on the tip. Are they there? Can
you see them, all tiny over there on the end
of your finger? Now that you have them over
there, barely bigger than a peanut, can you
also imagine just how squeaky and high-
pitched their voice has become, now that
they are so very small?

[ALL *look intently at their middle finger; ROBYN
drops left arm, raises right.*]

Now that they're way over there on the tip of your finger speaking in that silly, tiny squeaky voice, I want you to hear them saying all those nasty things again-the excuses, lies, false promises, and criticisms-but whenever they speak, whatever it is they say, make sure they are saying it in their tiny squeaky voice. And now if you want to, you can give them a new name, something really silly. There's no judgment, just whatever comes to mind. Nadia?

NADIA: [*Nervous smile playing on her lips.*] I'm calling her Frosty and she's saying, "You better join the gym or you'll end up as fat as your mum."

[*Intake of breath from ALL; ROBYN tuts disapproval.*]

RUTH: Is there anything you'd like to say to her now?

NADIA: [*Frowning, bullish.*] You are wrong, I'm nothing like my mother. You think you'll be happier with *her*, but you won't be, and-by the way-you're the one who needs the fucking gym.

IRENE: [*Confidently rising, unleashing her middle finger as if it's spring-loaded.*] You're

a stupid bitch. [*Pause.*] You're a stupid
bitch. [*Pitch of voice rising.*] You're a
stupid bitch. [NADIA *and* ROBYN *gasp.*]

RUTH: What is his new name, Irene?

IRENE: Lucifer.

RUTH: Is there anything you'd like to say to him
         now?

IRENE: Go to hell.

[ALL *laugh;* IRENE *bows and sits, flushed.*]

RUTH: Eshe?

ESHE: [*Face scrunched, fiddling with silver
         cross, hesitant.*] I can't do it. I don't
         want to mock him like that.

RUTH: That's okay, Eshe. This is just a
         technique, and one of many we'll be using
         that can help reduce their hold over you. We
         can come back to it later if you'd like?

[*Long pause;* ESHE *twists cross; room falls silent.*]

ESHE: I think I can do the name bit . . .
         It's . . . Ball Sack. [*Relieved.*]

RUTH: [*Smiling.*] That's a big step, Eshe, well
done.

[*Pause.*]

Robyn?

ROBYN: [*Glaring hard at the tip of her finger,
voice like she's inhaled helium.*] I'm
leaving you for someone fun who's not
riddled with disease.

[ALL *silent, unsure whether to laugh or cry.*]

RUTH: And his name?

ROBYN: [*With conviction.*] Voldemort.

RUTH: Is there anything you'd like to say to him
now?

ROBYN: Yeah, there is. Fuck you and your "soulful
love" bullshit. [ALL *laugh in relief.*]

LIN: [*Rising to her feet without prompt, arm
extended with purpose.*] You're mad, bad,
and sad.

RUTH: And his name?

LIN: Dick Dust.

RUTH: What would you like to say to him now?

LIN: [*Nodding.*] You're not worthy of my love.

[ESHE *looks to* RUTH *and stands.*]

RUTH: When you're ready, Eshe.

ESHE: [*Slowly, deliberately extending her finger.*] What's wrong with you? This place is a pigsty. I'm not putting up with it anymore.

[*Sharp intake from* ALL.]

RUTH: [*Gently.*] Is there anything you'd like to say to them now?

ESHE: You're a liar and a cheat. You're no good!

[ALL *clap.*]

RUTH: Reader, are you ready to have a go?

[*Pause.*]

Okay, great. So now every time the voice of your heartbreaker comes to mind, you know what to do . . . give them the finger.

CHAPTER 6

Radical Acceptance

The Art of Letting Go

Soon enough you will find yourself back in the intrusive rumination cycle, trying once again to work it all out, plotting heinous punishments for your ex—bringing them down, destroying them. Don't judge yourself for doing this. Take a deep breath and read these words aloud:

Things are not as I want them to be,
Nor as they should be.
They are as they are.

This is radical acceptance,[1] and it is a choice we can make both in the moment and as an ongoing process. It's an acceptance of what is *as it is*. This is not the same as approval or resignation, and it's not forgiveness or surrender; radical acceptance is never a passive act. It's a downing of tools, a conscious, active decision not to struggle anymore. What has happened has happened and no amount of struggling with it will change that.

And let's face it, radical times need radical solutions.

Radical because it means going all the way; it's a total acceptance of the fundamental and complete nature of the situation and all that has led to it, without exceptions or caveats. *Radical* because the consequences are far-reaching and the change generated is felt at the deepest level. *Radical* because radicals advocate for change and are often revolutionary.

In Hindi, *radical* means fiery and fierce. We like the juxtaposition of fiery and fierce with *acceptance* because it changes its energy into something altogether more powerful and alive. It bestows upon *radical* a seismic quality that it deserves.

We don't usually think of acceptance as being a precursor to change, but it is. It is the intentional act of accepting what has already happened so that you can clear a space to think about what's next.

Betrayal creates a dialectical tension where two things exist together even though they seem to contradict one another: I love them and hate them; I want to stay and go; I want to kill them and kiss them; they are my safe and my dangerous person. Trying to resolve this tension leads to deadlock. But radically accepting the natural presence of this unavoidable tension releases you from the pressure to eliminate it.

Acknowledge and accept that the unjustified, unfair, monstrous thing has happened, and that however much you try to think your way out of it, it is now in your life. We are inviting you to incorporate it into your life rather than keep fighting against it. In accepting this, you are also accepting all the things that happened before this moment, including your part in them. Nothing in the past can be changed, and it has all led to this moment, which also can't be changed.

Let this sink in.

Imagine you have an important meeting at 9 a.m. and the bus you're on is stuck in traffic; it looks like you're going to be late. You have two choices. You can fight it and be angry, worry about the consequences of your lateness, stress about the fact that you're stressed . . . enter into yet another round of the rumination battle to figure it out, restore justice, punish the perpetrator (or the bus driver). Or . . . you can radically accept it, and as the bus inches forward, distract your mind and turn up the tunes. The bus will be late either way, but only one route offers a path to peace.

Radical acceptance doesn't change the facts; it changes the outcome. Your heart rate goes down, your body releases its tension, your breathing slows, and you can begin to restore balance to mind and body. In *this* state of being, we are powerful—in spite of what has happened.

How much energy have you spent resisting it, agonizing over the "What ifs?," trying to figure out "Why me?"?

That very question is predicated on the idea that the world is fair and just. That bad things don't happen to good people, that good things shouldn't happen to bad people. This is not how it is. Why you? Why *not* you?

We all fall into this trap; it's a human way of trying to make sense of a complex world. But unfortunately, bad things can happen to anyone. If you radically accept the radically unfair, even though it may make no sense, you will set yourself free. Radical acceptance represents the start of a new way of being.

> *Things are not as I want them to be,*
> *Nor as they should be.*
> *They are as they are.*

Learn it by heart and have it on repeat.

The Troll and the Hole

Imagine you're in a game of tug-of-war with your heartbreak.[2] You hold one end of the rope, and on the other end is a scary-looking troll who represents all your unwanted thoughts and feelings. Between you and the troll is a huge black hole and you sense that it contains something awful. Maybe it's a crocodile? Maybe it's a snake? Or maybe it's an endless spinning into existential nothingness?

So, you keep fighting, holding on to that rope, not giving in an inch, terrified of both the hole and the troll. Your hand is sore, you're very thirsty, possibly in need of a snack, and you're not sure how much longer you can keep going.

But there is a way out of this exhausting and frightening situation, which you haven't yet turned your mind to, so hard have you been trying to win.

Let go of the rope.

Because when you let go, no one goes near the hole. Instead, you fall backward, dust yourself off, and walk away to get on with something else. All the energy you have been expending in the tug-of-war is freed up.

You win by letting go of the struggle. And when you do, your thoughts are released, just as you are. Much like radical acceptance, the resolution lies in doing the opposite of what you might expect.

It's also important to manage expectations. Even though you might have promised yourself you'll practice radical acceptance, you will forget, or find yourself not wanting to do it, and you will inevitably fall into the trap of trying to figure it all out again.

That's okay. Gently notice when this happens and remind your-self that you are probably trying to resolve the dialectic tension of betrayal—and feel very clever in the process.

If you need more convincing, try half an hour of intense strug-gle, ruminate your heart out, and then half an hour of radical ac-ceptance. Which felt better?

By now you will have noticed that most of the exercises you have been introduced to center around going with and letting go. This may not be how you are used to op-erating. If you are feeling uncomfortable with the idea, remember "Dropping Anchor" will help to build a sense of safety as you move forward. Know that you can do it whenever you wish, to help your body and spirit relax.

In choosing to radically accept what has happened, you cease to give your energy to someone who has broken your heart and can use it instead to reignite your flame within and create the possibility that you are more powerful and freer than you ever imagined. That you are an enormous force for good, and an agent for change who can define yourself according to what is important—as *you* see it.

CHAPTER 7

The Vow of Silence

Your brain is trying to process what has happened and why. But as we know, rumination offers only false promises; it's a ghoulish masquerade. What your rumination is really doing is helping you avoid the real and awful undercurrent: that you have been heartbroken. Of course, you would rather avoid that, but remember: the rumination is your jailer, not your friend. The journey to freedom can only begin once you stop struggling with what has happened. We know this is hard, and so to help you with it, we're inviting you now to take a vow of silence. It is a moratorium on talking about your heartbreaker for the time that you are with us, and it acts as a rumination container. It also represents the moment we turn away from them and keep the focus firmly on you. The reality is that your heartbreaker is irrelevant to your onward journey. You will want to speak of them, and you can, but when you do, reminding yourself that you took this vow will present you again with a choice of where to redirect your energy—back toward the heartbreaker or ... onward toward yourself.

You will most likely need to keep on taking this vow, and that's okay. It's not about nailing it from the get-go, but about a wholehearted commitment to give it your best shot—and to keep on trying.

Say after me ...

"From this moment forward, I vow not to talk about my heartbreaker. I will keep the focus firmly on myself so that I may flourish and grow."

You will have feelings about this. Notice them; see if you can name them. Feelings have a reliable arc: they reach a moment of highest intensity, inevitably peak, and then subside—it may *feel* overwhelming, but it won't actually overwhelm you. Go *with* the feeling rather than fight against it.

Riptides are pockets in the sea where the current is going in the opposite direction to what you'd expect. You might swim out from the beach, then turn around and try to swim back, only to find that the tide is now pulling you farther out. You try to swim harder and faster, but you're going nowhere, and the panic rises. You must get back to the shore! But if you keep swimming against the tide, you will continue to get nowhere. The only thing that happens is you exhaust yourself.

What you need to do is take a leap of faith and let the tide take you farther out to sea. Once you are released from the riptide, you can swim around it safely and then head back to shore.

Struggling against your feelings means living in fear that they will overwhelm you if you let them come, and this fear alone will intensify their potency and leave you with double trouble—the feeling *and* the fear of the feeling.

It's only through letting your feelings be that you discover this.

It's natural to fear that your feelings will drown you, but they won't, not if you go with them. We are conditioned to escape danger and negative states through suppressing, denying, numbing, getting away, and scrambling for solutions. And all of these strategies are needed, sometimes. But if you let yourself feel—and yes, you will experience the intensity of your feelings—you will also learn that it won't go on forever. It will always inevitably subside. Problems are created when you consistently shut your feelings off, guard against them, and live with anxiety about when they might come back. If you act to get rid of them before the peak—by drinking, distracting, or solving—you don't ever get to the other side.

The desire to avoid painful feelings through distraction and rumination is strong and difficult to resist, which is why you have taken this vow until you have finished reading this book. From now on, if you need to mention them at all, you can either use the name you created for them when you gave them the finger or refer to them as your "unmentionable."

PART II

The Past

CHAPTER 8

Bonding Blueprints

Almost without exception, humans have a deep and primal need to feel connected to the people, places, and systems that surround them. Buried deep within our genomes,[1] the need to feel accepted, respected, included, and loved is as fundamental as the need for food and shelter. Siblings, parents, friends, teachers, the wider community, they all have a bearing on our sense of security and belonging, and ultimately how we feel about ourselves—and like a golden thread stretching back to our earliest days, these first relationships create the bonding blueprints for all subsequent ones.

What was your early nest like? Was it soft and cozy like a hummingbird's or sturdy and large like an eagle's? Who was in it with you? Was there a big noisy brood or just you? What were the sounds and smells, the atmosphere? Was life predictable—did you know what to expect—or was it chaotic and scary? What was the ecosystem around it like—the social and cultural messages that influenced how you felt about the world? Take a moment to write down your thoughts.

Your experience in the early nest gave rise to fledgling beliefs about how the world works, acting like an internal map to navigate all your relationships and experiences to come. Your brain's neural pathways are at their most active around the age of two,[2] firing on all cylinders, reorganizing and adapting themselves in response to your experiences. Childhood is a very busy time of meaning making and pattern formation. It is when we start to decide things about ourselves, others, and the world. And these nascent understandings are powerful and persistent. Childhood is a time when you are figuring out not just whether other people can be trusted, but also your sense of your own worth.

While much of your internal map has helped guide you into becoming the person you are today, some of the information contained in those early fledgling beliefs may be clipping your wings and steering you off course. Because—

adaptable as we are as children—we don't yet have a full arsenal of understanding to comprehend the complexities of adult relationships and the world around us.

You may not wish to go back and look at your childhood. We have this in mind and will go gently.

*   *   *

Heartbreak represents an interpersonal rupture, one that can activate our past knowledge and experience of others and ourselves. When the bond is broken, we try to mitigate the distress and our internal map is triggered into action. Our early bonding blueprints are activated, and it's worth taking a closer look at these because they can influence not just how much distress we feel when we are heartbroken, but also our perceptions of ourselves and our partners.

Our intention is to use the full power of your adult mind to take another look at what was happening in your early nest, to understand how you made sense of it back then, and to shine an empathetic and understanding adult perspective on it, so that you have everything you need to ride out this storm with confidence. Feelings may come up as we go along. Remember: they are important, you need them.

Picture this...

Back in the 1960s, American psychologist Harry Harlow conducted a series of shockingly cruel experiments on a group of baby rhesus macaque monkeys.[3] The baby monkeys were removed from their mothers shortly after birth and put alone in a cage with two inanimate "mother" substitutes, one covered with soft cozy cloth and the other made of bare wire but with a bottle of milk attached.

Harlow was interested to see which need the monkeys prioritized: the need for food or the need for comfort. The babies went straight to the cozy look-alike, even when they were hungry.

As if this setup wasn't brutal enough, the researchers then removed the cuddly "mother" and replaced her with a teddy bear that made loud scary noises. And even though the wiry "mother" was present, the terrified baby macaques didn't reach for her. Instead, they screamed and crouched in fear, covering their heads, sucking their thumbs, and rocking back and forth.

Harlow's experiments demonstrated that, without comfort, baby macaque monkeys couldn't regulate their fear. The monkeys who grew up with these fake mothers found it hard to know how to cope. They were timid and struggled to stand up for themselves, less curious, and had more difficulty mating and making friends—in short, they felt unsafe. And they did what they needed to do to feel safer: they became submissive and hid themselves away in order not to be harmed. And it worked for a while, until they got bigger and were put in more complex environments, where they doubled down on their original strategy of self-subordination. But rather than making them safe, the unintended consequences of their strategy was that they were vulnerable to being picked on. Not because there was anything wrong with them, but because what had happened to them at the hands of Harlow meant that they had learned to respond to unsafe situations by being unthreatening. And far from making them safer, it made them more vulnerable to those who might take advantage.

These unethical experiments marked a turning point away from the Victorian idea that to comfort children was to spoil them and that their emotional needs were irrelevant, paving the way for attachment theory[4]—the idea that infants need reassurance and comfort from a responsive caregiver to feel safe, and that the extent to which they receive these forms the bonding blueprint by which they navigate all future relationships, long after they've flown the nest.

Early bonding blueprints act as an emotional mapping system, giving us coordinates to navigate the relational world with a sense of predictability and safety. If we didn't have them, we'd be very much at sea. It is only once we spread our wings, leave the nest, and take to the open skies that these beliefs and strategies are put to the test.

If your map hasn't been updated for a while, this is a good moment to take a closer look—after all, who isn't frustrated when an outdated GPS fails to let them know the road ahead is closed?

If you were lucky enough to have had an early nest where your caregivers were responsive to your young needs, you will have felt more or less secure and developed a bonding blueprint that reflects this. Your emotional regulation system will be well developed, and you can use it to navigate choppy waters. Growing up with a warm and caring atmosphere around you and having your needs met and your feelings valued will have given you a sense of safety growing up. You will feel settled and calm in relationships, and intimacy and commitment will feel good. You are likely to have a strong and solid sense of yourself, be able to negotiate conflict well, be emotionally stable, and manage the ups and downs of relationships with relative ease. Power struggles are rare, and you are generally supportive and empathetic and able to ask for help when you need it. You tend toward feeling sunny and safe. You are the **Safe Harbors**.[5]

If your early caregivers were unresponsive to your emotional—and perhaps physical—needs, you will have felt insecure and unsafe in your early nest. You will have tried out all your available emotional responses, but quickly learned that in the unsafe environment—just like the monkeys—some responses kept you safer than others. And we all hold on very tightly to what keeps us feeling safe, so these strategies can be highly resistant to change, even when different strategies might work better. For some, this might mean avoiding getting too close—the **Lone Rangers**.[6] For others, it might be trying to stay very close—the **Close Rangers**.[7] Or some of you might not be sure whether it's safer to be close or distant—the **Roller Rangers**.[8]

Let's take a closer look...

Lone Rangers. If you are self-reliant and independent in relationships and feel uncomfortable if the emotional temperature gets too hot, you may be a Lone Ranger. While able to be warm and loving, Lone Rangers can find the challenges of intimacy threatening. Emotional closeness reveals their deeper feelings and, under pressure, can leave them wanting to flee—it can't be trusted, so better to keep away. Conflict can feel threatening too, and Lone Rangers tend to be evasive and distant to guard against feeling unsafe. Their early nests were characterized by a lack of responsiveness from their caregivers *or* by overcontrolling, overbearing ones. So ultimately, Lone Rangers do what they need to do to keep safe—develop the protective strategies of self-sufficiency and independence. If emotional proximity feels overwhelming and you hate the idea of being tied down (except perhaps to the bedposts), this could be you. A classic Lone Ranger might respond to the question "How come you've never settled down?" with "I just haven't met the right person." In this way, Lone Rangers center the problem outside of themselves and avoid exposing their own vulnerability. Often unaware of their own distress, they tend to suppress their attachment needs and seek independence to regulate their experience. Their blueprint mapping system looks a bit like this:

If I keep my distance, then I will be safe.

Close Rangers. If you are sensitive to rejection and fear-ful of bonds breaking, like to keep people nearby, are vigi-lant to changes in emotional temperature, and need a fair bit of reassurance that things are all okay, you may be a Close Ranger. Their early caregiving was responsive, but not predictably so: sometimes it was great, sometimes it wasn't, sometimes people met your needs, and sometimes they didn't. It was uncertain, and so it was important for you to stay close and alert. And unlike the Lone Rangers, Close Rangers tend to center the problem within, finding fault and blaming themselves. They can be independent and fun-loving, but when they sense conflict, separation, or rejection, the strategies they use to cope with the dis-tress involve seeking greater proximity. They become focused on reestablishing emotional closeness and rumi-nating on worst-case scenarios.[9]

Imagine you meet up with your Close Ranger buddy just after they've had a first date.

"How did it go? Did you have fun?" you ask.

"I've texted her three times since I left the restaurant, but she hasn't written back, so obviously she isn't in-terested. Should I text again?" the Close Ranger might reply.

The Close Ranger needs contact to be reassured that all is well. Their blueprint mapping system looks a bit like this:

If *I stay close,* then *I will feel safe.*

Roller Rangers. If early caregiving was unpredictably responsive but with an added dimension of danger and punishment—when the "safe" person could also be "dangerous"—children grow up on uncertain footing. Part Lone and part Close, the Roller Rangers can experience relationships as tumultuous and, at times, bewildering. They find it hard to know where they stand, whether to trust or not, and how to read the safety signals, and so relationships can feel hard to navigate. If you find it tricky to make sense of what's what in relationships, not sure whether to stay close or run for the hills, you may be in this camp. Their blueprint mapping system looks a bit like this:

If *I stay vigilant,* then *I will be safe.*

It bears mentioning here that the experience of being betrayed can temporarily mimic the Roller Ranger experience—the safe person has, in a sudden turn, become dangerous, leaving you feeling bemused and disoriented.

*　　*　　*

When Lone Rangers and Close Rangers get together, the push and pull of wanting and not wanting can create intense moments of connection but equally intense moments of pain. One wants more and the other wants less; closeness frightens one, distance frightens the other . . .

First date: the Lone Ranger is complimentary and self-assured, asking questions because this is comfortable territory in which they don't have to get too close. The Close Ranger finds this attractive as it indicates interest in them and a reassuring proximity—they want to be close. And so the dance begins. The Lone Ranger enjoys the excitement of the emerging relationship. Who doesn't? But once it looks as if it's heading toward commitment, echoes of their past templates are heard. They withdraw. But while the Lone Ranger is heading for the hills (often running), the Close Ranger has become anxious, grabs the binoculars, gathers the hounds, and calls in the SWAT team.

Roller Rangers too may take to the hills—also at quite a pace—but soon start to feel lost because they don't have any snacks and have left their compass behind. So back home they go. If their partner is *also* a roller ranger, they might return to find the fridge empty and the car gone. Neither knows what's going on or where the other is. But if both parties just stay put and ride out their feelings of uncertainty, eventually they'll end up back at the ranch together and can settle down.

The key to success within all these pairings is solid communication. The Lone Rangers among you could always leave a note before running off, and the Close Rangers could relax and read it.

I need some alone time.
I love you.
Back at 6 p.m.

While all this is going on, the Safe Harbors among you are looking on bemused at the comings and goings and wondering what all the fuss is about, but trusting it'll get resolved in time. The Safe Harbor knows that their Lone Ranger lover needs their alone time and will come back to them when they've had enough space, and that the Close Ranger needs a hug and reassurance. The Roller Ranger lover can circle round and round their Safe Harbor—who won't bat an eyelid.

So, if you're running for the hills, waiting for the SWAT team to respond, or tired and in need of that snack, try communicating your needs—with words. And if you find the Safe Harbors a little overly reliable in their ability to meet your needs, and somewhat lacking in the chemistry department (where's the dopamine hit?), don't overlook or dismiss them out of hand, because they might be just who you need—not only to feel safe, but to be safe.

*   *   *

At this point you may be trying to figure out which of these patterns fits you best. Humans don't naturally slot into neat categories—perhaps you have the capacity to feel more secure with certain people or in certain communities, while with others, no matter how hard you try, you always feel on unsure footing. For the moment, focus on the relationship that has brought you here, and see if you can hear echoes of any of these patterns within it.

All of us develop early strategies to keep us feeling safe and confident within the dynamics of our relationships. They usually have a conditional ring to them—*if... then...* You may resonate with the strategies you've just heard from the Rangers, but yours may have a different flavor or emphasis, or an added specificity to them. See if you can identify what yours might be... have a go. Here are some examples:

If I do what I'm told, *then* my parents won't be angry.

If I keep my feelings to myself, *then* I won't be teased.

If I stay in control, *then* there won't be any nasty surprises.

If I make people laugh, *then* they will be happy.

If I do what other people want, *then* I won't be rejected.

If I behave more like my sister, *then* I will be loved.

If I get angry, *then* I'll be punished.

Helpful as they were when you were young, these protective strategies can outlive their usefulness, and as we find ourselves in new situations, they can become restrictive, limiting our range of options to meet the needs of different social and emotional contexts.

CHAPTER 9

The Dark Triad

There is one situation, however, where knowing your attachment pattern and protective strategies will provide you with no guidance... or protection. Because there are some people—charming, attractive, and powerful—who are not playing by the usual rules. They are playing the game of the Dark Triad, the unholiest of unholy trinities—narcissism, psychopathy, and Machiavellianism[1]—a major relationship red flag.[2]

Narcissism

Psychopathy   Machiavellianism

Very few people meet the clinical criteria for any one of these three, let alone the full triumvirate, thank God. But the more of these traits that any individual possesses, the further away they are from the rule book. In fact, some of them have ripped it up completely and chucked it in the bin (or in your face)!

Narcissists, with an inflated sense of their own importance and a deep need for admiration and attention, hijack relationships with their high demands and impossible standards. Some narcissists present as very self-confident and demanding (grandiose narcissism), but some as self-conscious, withdrawn, and fragile-seeming (vulnerable or covert narcissism), but underneath these differing styles is the same entitlement, superiority, and antagonism.

Those on the psychopathic end are often highly intelligent, superficially charming, grandiose, and manipulative. They tend to lack the capacity for remorse and shame, often ending relationships with little difficulty. (What's not to love?)

The Machiavels are a cunning and nasty bunch, duplicitous, scheming, and unscrupulous. Indifferent to basic morality, they are often ruthlessly ambitious and will stop at nothing to get what they want.

No one sets out to fall for one of this lot…

But here's the thing. They are often extremely flattering, impressive, sexually confident, charming, well groomed, and sometimes even rich and powerful. They make you believe it's you and them against the world, like Bonnie and Clyde (one hopes without the killings). They're the punchy types who think nothing of plugging their number into your phone, grabbing your coat, and saying, "Congratulations, you've pulled."

People with this trinity of traits can often come labeled as "The One" on account of the high chemistry they create, and when they turn their attention on you, it can be very difficult to resist. But it is a chemistry that rarely signifies love-ever-after, despite the strong feelings to the contrary. Perhaps unsurprisingly, they are more predisposed to infidelity than others.[3]

And they are exceptionally good at lying, something the rest of us are notoriously bad at detecting. If you have been berating yourself for not spotting the signs sooner, for not reading clues, for not having suspicions that those late work drinks or trips abroad were anything other than innocent, and indeed for choosing the heartbreaker in the first place, you are not alone. These expert manipulators can go on weaving their intricate webs of deceit over months and years without detection. If they weren't able to charm and deceive, they might find themselves with few friends. They can more easily manage the physical symptoms that accompany their deceptions too—sweating, fidgeting, darting eyes. While most of us are more of the "leaky liar" type,[4] these experts can conceal their falsehood beneath a veneer of charm and seduction that would fool anyone.

So, if you fell in love with one of these charming love-bombers, don't judge yourself. And if you're not sure whether you're with one, here are some key pointers:

You have stopped seeing your friends and family.

You feel repeatedly insecure.

Your needs are not being considered.

You're wondering whether you've lost your mind.

Your version of events is being constantly undermined.

You want to end the relationship, but it feels impossible.

If you've identified with anything on this list (or everything on it), the first thing to know is that you are not alone and you are not losing your mind. But you may be with someone who, no matter how hard you try or wish it were otherwise, is never going to meet your needs. Bringing this into awareness for the very first time may be scary, even shocking, or perhaps there is a sense of relief. Whatever comes up for you, don't judge it, let it be. We're here to help you navigate your way through this.

CHAPTER 10

Identity

Before we continue, please make sure that you have that photo of yourself from when you were a kid.

Now, we're going to travel back in time for the next little while, but before we do we would like you to create a safe place that will help you to feel grounded as we go on.

Find a comfortable position either sitting or lying down, with your head, neck, and spine aligned. Uncross your legs and let your hands rest in your lap or by your sides. We're going to ask you to use your imagination to create a place of deep relaxation and stillness.

Okay, let's begin by taking a few easy breaths, breathing in and breathing all the way out. Breathe in again, and this time see if you can send the warm energy of the breath to any part of your body that is tense, sore, or tight, and then release the tension with the exhale, breathing it all the way out. Do this a few times until you start to relax.

Any emotions and thoughts that are rocking around can be acknowledged and calmed with the breath, so that your emotional self is still and quiet, like a lake with no ripples.

Now imagine a place where you feel calm and peaceful and easy, a place from your past or somewhere you've always wanted to go. It doesn't matter where, just as long as it's a place that feels good and safe and peaceful. Allow the place to become real in your mind's eye. Look around and take it all in: the colors, the scenery, the smells and sounds. Close your eyes for a few minutes if that helps. Feel the safety and peace of the place soaking into your skin, through the muscle and bone, all the way down to each and every cell, reaching the stillness at your very core.

Know that you can come back to this place of safety in your mind, whenever you wish to help your body and spirit relax, simply by getting into a comfortable position and imagining yourself there.

*   *   *

So with your journal in hand, find somewhere comfortable to sit. We want you to think back to a time before you were ten years old when things felt difficult. And as you do, take a couple of long, deep breaths, in through your nose and out through your mouth, and allow all the tension to leave your body. Give yourself permission to relax. For a minute or two, just observe your breath, noticing how your belly rises on the inhale and falls back down as you breathe out. Allow your breath to flow freely, bringing you to a place of stillness. There is no rush: just be with your breath and observe the movements of your belly up and down. Allow any thoughts to come up and pass without judgment. All is well.

Think of the memory now, and as you do, we'd like you to see your younger self in this memory as if you were watching her on a television screen. Describe what you see in as much detail as you can. What is she doing? Who is she with? What is happening? What is she feeling? Give yourself time so the scene really comes alive.

Deep within you, the young girl you once were is waiting for you. She had needs that were not met and that you have long forgotten. She needed to feel safe and loved, to feel that she mattered and that she could be herself.

Now we'd like you to imagine walking into the scene as the adult you are now: go and stand near her, and introduce yourself. Tell her how pleased you are to see her, and gently ask her how she's feeling.

She's about to tell you something important; she's about to tell you how she feels about herself. Listen carefully, because she may find it difficult.

What is she telling you? (*I am...*) Write the words down.

Bending down to her height now, and with all the warmth and compassion you can muster, tell her that you know she's been doing her best, that it's been really confusing for her, and that you have something to say about how you see her.

What did you tell her? (*You are...*) Write the words down.

How does she respond? What is the expression on her face? Does she say anything?

Take some time to enjoy this connection with her. You can let her know that you will always be there for her.

When you're ready, gently bring your awareness back to your breath and the sensations in your body. Take your time. You've just done something important, generous, and kind.

In that memory, the way you felt as a young girl represents the fledgling belief you developed about yourself. What your adult self told her is a new, flying belief infused with understanding and empathy—altogether more representative of who you are. As an adult, you are able to see what your younger self couldn't see back then: that it wasn't her fault, that she was doing her best, and that she couldn't understand it all because she was only a child.

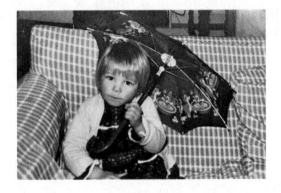

Alice

Take some time to write down your memory and identify what your younger self thought about herself (fledgling belief) and what you as an adult told her about herself (flying belief). What have you done in your life to manage the fledgling belief and keep you feeling safe? What kind of protective strategies did you develop? How might this have helped and hindered you in your life so far? We're

Ruth

going to take a look now at your fellow guests' childhood memories and explore what was going on for them, how they navigated their close relationships, and what strategies they developed to cope.

*   *   *

Before we go on, coming up next is one of those "Dropping Anchor" moments we mentioned at the start of the book. If you're feeling upset by hearing the other women's stories as we go along, or in thinking about your own, remember that you can always drop anchor to ground yourself.

*   *   *

Eshe's memory:

Eshe is eight or nine and dancing in the yard with
her younger sister. Their parents are having a barbecue.
There's music playing and everyone is happy. People are
smoking and drinking. She's holding hands with her sister,
leaning back and spinning round and round, going faster
and faster. All of a sudden, there is a sharp pain to
Eshe's head and she's on the ground and people are
staring at her. Her dad rushes over and yanks her up,
drags her inside by her hair, and everything goes deathly
quiet. Eshe braces herself, covers her face. She knows
what's coming: a hard thwack to her head, and he's
shouting that she's ruined the party. She puts her hand
to her face. Blood drips from her fingers; his ring must
have caught her nose. She feels dizzy and faint and
scared. Her dad is shouting at her to go to her room and
stay there. Up in the bedroom, Eshe wants to lie down
but is afraid she might stain the bedding, so she takes a
tissue and presses it against her nose to stop the bleeding
and throbbing. She is shaking with pain and fear. She's
angry too, with herself, with everyone, but most of all
with her father. But as the bleeding subsides and she
calms down, she starts to berate herself for being so
clumsy; she blames herself. Why does she always ruin
everything? She must try harder and not make her dad
so angry. She vows never to let something like this happen
again.

Eshe's early life was chaotic much of the time, and her father's drinking made him unpredictable and aggressive. She was never quite sure what his mood would be, but knew that more often than not his anger would escalate into violence. She was too young to understand then that he was an alcoholic, and she did her best to smooth things over and avoid punishment. She blamed herself, because at least this way she had some sense of control over the situation: if it was her fault, then she could make it better by being and doing better. But the truth of it was that she was feeling alone, unloved, and inadequate, because she couldn't make it stop. Perhaps nobody noticed because on the outside she was good at appearing calm and cheerful, as though nothing could touch her, but inside she felt frightened and vulnerable, unsure whether anyone was there for her at all.

She told grown-up Eshe that she felt she was "no good, and it's my fault that bad things happen."

She developed a sensitive warning system to changes in atmosphere, and although she didn't always know what was needed, she tried not to make things worse and to always appear cheerful so her dad wouldn't get angry.

If I'm careful, *then* things won't get worse.

If I'm cheerful, *then* people won't be angry.

Grown-up Eshe extended this strategy into her adult relationships and her intimate relationship with her betrayer, to gain a semblance of control.

And her strategies did keep her safe most of the time, but trying to keep the peace all the time meant her own needs disappeared from view and she became more and more lost, exhausted, and disconnected from herself. And people didn't stop being angry. And when they did get angry at her, instead of calling time on the relationship, or leaving, she kept on trying to smooth things over and de-escalate situations to make things safe.

When Eshe met her younger self, she told her that she was lovable, that she needed to be safe, and that it wasn't her fault. She told her little self that she was important and could ask for help.

Eshe

Fledgling belief: I'm no good, and it's my fault that bad things happen.

Protective strategy: If I'm careful, then things won't get worse. If I'm cheerful, then people won't be angry.

Unintended consequence: I feel lost and disconnected and exhausted.

Flying belief: I'm lovable. It's not my fault. I'm important and can ask for help.

Robyn's memory:

Robyn is nine and her mother is holding up a large packet of sweets. Robyn's eyes are searching out the label, keen to identify which sweets they are, hoping they're her favorites—rhubarb and custard—but then she sees her mother's face looking like thunder and realizes something is wrong because she only gets sweets on her birthday . . . and it's still May. And then it comes, her mother accusing her of stealing them from the shop . . . but she's never seen this packet of sweets. Her stomach tightens in knots. She tells her mum she didn't steal the sweets, but her mother is convinced and claims she found the packet inside Robyn's school satchel and shows her exactly where. Robyn knows she didn't put them in there and knows she didn't steal them. Her mother is now ushering her out of the house, saying she has to take them back and apologize to the shopkeeper. As Robyn passes the stairs, she looks up to see her brother smirking. She starts to say something, but her mother snaps at her to be quiet. Ben is two years older and has a temper to equal their mother's. Robyn knows protest is hopeless: he can do no wrong in their mother's eyes. She's been here many, many times before. Ten minutes later they are standing in front of the shopkeeper, and her mother places the sweet packet on the counter and demands Robyn explain herself. Robyn knows it'll be over if she says sorry, but she's damned if she's going to apologize for something she hasn't even done. She looks at the ceiling and then to the ground and imagines herself disappearing. Face and cheeks burning up, she turns on her heel and runs off, without looking back.

Robyn did what she needed to do to protect herself. She disconnected from those around her and over time from herself. She grew up feeling helpless to advocate for herself and her truth, always batted it away, bullied by her brother and blamed by her mother. In her memory she told adult Robyn that she was feeling all alone and had no one on her side, that there was something bad about her—otherwise why would everyone be so unkind to her? As she grew up, she spent more and more time away from home or shutting herself off. She avoided other people to avoid getting hurt. As she entered adulthood, she discovered that alcohol made her feel better and helped her navigate the challenges of socializing, particularly the emotional challenges of intimate relationships. But the unintended consequence of her withdrawal into alcohol was that she remained disconnected from those around her, a disconnection that ultimately hurt her more than it helped. She was always on the fringe of things and was left by her unmentionable for the very strategy she'd employed to stay safe: being distant. When adult Robyn spoke to her younger self, she told her that she understood why she was scared and lonely. She created a flying belief for her little self—that Robyn's feelings were important, that she was brave and good.

Robyn

Fledgling belief: I'm alone, no one's on my side, and I'm bad.

Protective strategy: If I disconnect and withdraw from others, then I won't be hurt.

Unintended consequence: But now I'm always on the outside feeling even more lonely and still being hurt.

Flying belief: My feelings matter, and I am brave and good.

Nadia's memory:

Nadia is six and her dad is taking her on an outing to his office in a huge building where he is a biology lecturer. It's the weekend and the building is empty. She is so happy to be there with him, just the two of them. There are two desks in his office, one for him and one for the other lecturer who Nadia hasn't met but has heard about. Nadia's dad has a chair that turns all the way around, and she's kicking off the ground and flying round on it. She is pretending to be a grown-up, answering the phone and pressing all the buttons so they light up.

A man comes in and Nadia feels something change. He is wearing a striped suit and thick glasses; Nadia thinks he must be very important and clever. Then she notices a boy who has come in with him. He's wearing a suit too, just like his dad's. How silly, Nadia is thinking. The important man is talking with her dad in low whispers. Nadia has no idea what they're talking about. The boy is now in the corner of the office examining a human skeleton and rattling off names of bones. Nadia hasn't heard of a lot of them, and he's oozing so much confidence over there in his suit, like a tiny teacher. The man is praising him, and her dad is now too: how clever he is to have remembered all those names. "Maybe you'll be a professor one day," his dad says to him.

Nadia's dad turns to her, points to his head, and says, "You know this one."

Nadia knows because it's the head, of course, but then thinks maybe it has another name. Yes, it does, but she's forgotten it, so she says, "It's your head."

The boy laughs.

Her dad frowns but says encouragingly, "Yes, but what's the bony structure called?"

"Face?" she offers tentatively, knowing already that she has got it wrong.

The boy announces, "Skull," and Nadia wants to disappear.

She pinches her hand hard under the desk to distract herself from the heat rising in her body. She wants to scream and doesn't know what to do. She's feeling crushed and it's all the more acute because she had felt so confident and happy in the moments leading up to it.

On the way home, her dad doesn't say anything about the other man or the boy or the skeleton, and he doesn't mention it to her mum either when they get home. She's thinking he's pretending it didn't happen and that he's embarrassed and disappointed with her. Nadia is unsure whether to mention it or not. She is feeling stupid for messing up, and she's feeling terrible for letting her dad down in front of the clever man she felt it was important to impress.

To keep anything like this from happening again, she develops the protective strategy of asking lots of questions, knowing that her dad likes that, and in this way she won't disappoint him. And it works: her parents tell her that curiosity is a wonderful quality, that it will serve her well in life, and she will go far. But inside she feels empty. Underneath all her questions, the experience at her dad's office settles into her—*I'm stupid*, she tells herself.

Nadia knows she is lucky to have kind parents who are planning on sending her to a good school. They really love her. They are good, and she's done something shameful, and maybe that means she doesn't deserve any of it. As she grows up, although people mostly seem pleased with her, underneath she is full of doubt and unsure of who she is or what she thinks—about anything.

Nadia was able to meet her younger self and tell her that she is capable, smart, and has her own voice—she's trying on this new flying belief. It's difficult as she's so used to asking questions, but the group is helping her, gently teasing when she keeps asking them, and in this way challenging Nadia to stay with the uncertainty and trust that she may already have the answer.

Nadia

Fledgling belief: I'm stupid and disappointing.

Protective strategy: If I ask lots of questions, no one will know I'm stupid and no one will be disappointed with me.

Unintended consequence: I'm always doubting myself and don't know who I am.

Flying belief: I am capable and smart, and I have a voice.

Irene's memory:

Irene is seven years old and it's her mother's birthday.
She's made a plan with her baby brother to make
their mom breakfast in bed as a birthday treat. They
have already been up to her bedroom with homemade
birthday cards, but she was fast asleep. It's now nearly
lunchtime and they are both in the kitchen. He's only a
babbling two-year-old, so isn't much help, but he loves
the sound the kettle makes when the water boils—
hissing and whistling like a steam train. The kettle is
blue and shiny. Irene loves that it's shiny and keeps it
polished so it stays that way. She's in charge; she's
always in charge these days. Her brother is crawling
around trying to mount the step stool Irene uses to
reach everything, but he keeps falling down onto his
bottom. He's such a baby, Irene thinks. The toast pops
and Irene is buttering two slices when she hears a
piercing screech. For a split second she thinks it's the
kettle . . . She spins round and drops the plate. Her
baby brother is howling and thrashing around on the
floor, his skin turning redder by the second. Then
she sees the empty kettle beside him on the floor—and
screams.

She can't move; it's as though her body is frozen.

Her mother comes hurtling down the stairs, shouting at her to get to the neighbors' house for help. Irene runs across the road, panicked and terrified, and the next thing she remembers, the ambulance is there, and her brother is being taken away along with her mum, still in her dressing gown. Irene thinks he's going to die. And when her mother doesn't come to pick her up from next door that night, she's sure he's dead, and she's sure it's her fault. When her mother returns to collect Irene the next day, she doesn't say anything about her brother and goes straight up to her bedroom. It's a day later that Irene finds out from the neighbor that her brother is still in the hospital but is alive; her mother isn't talking to her, and it remains that way for some time.

Irene was too young to understand then that her mother was depressed, not just because her father was so often away with the army—which is what she'd always say when Irene asked her what was wrong—but because he was having an affair and threatening her with divorce. Instead, Irene thought it must be her fault that her mother was so quiet and down, and it was certainly her fault that her brother was hurt. *I'm incompetent and can't be trusted,* she thought to herself, not able to understand that she should never have been put in that position of responsibility in the first place. She decided that she must be more careful, plan everything really well, and defer to others, who knew better than her.

And this felt safer. But this strategy had unintended consequences in her life and in her relationships. There was a kind of innocence to her. She never took any risks. And she undermined her own achievements, always claiming to be lucky rather than competent, and so never really *felt* capable—even though she clearly was. She rarely trusted her own feelings, and in her long marriage deferred to Stan; in doing so, she kept things stable, but often at the expense of her own needs and desires. She kept saying what a good life she'd had, and the group gently reminded Irene that she can have had a good life, *and* there could have been difficulties. The two statements can coexist— they'd say—reminding Irene of the dialectic.

What her older self saw and knew when she went back into the memory was that Irene was capable and full of fun and passion. Her brother's accident was not her fault, but nobody had told her that. She can trust herself; it was an accident.

Irene

Fledgling belief: I can't trust myself.

Protective strategy: If I'm careful and plan well, and if I defer to others, then everyone will be safe.

Unintended consequence: I don't feel capable or know what I want.

Flying belief: I am capable and full of fun and passion. I can trust myself.

Lin found the exercise too challenging, and she felt unable to go into any memory before the age of ten. She couldn't connect with who she was as a child and had no sense of what she might have been like. The group tried to help her create a picture of the little girl she once was, given the incredible woman she is now, but Lin just wept, unable to take in anything they said. None of it felt real or solid to her.

Lin approached Alice during the break and told her how wretched she is feeling, that she can't do it properly, and that she's now worried she won't get to where the other women have got to and won't feel any better when she leaves.

CHAPTER 11

Scene III

The Rabbit

Cozy den. Late next morning.

The women are gathered and ALICE turns to LIN.

ALICE: How about we start from a different place?
        How about you tell me what you liked doing
        as a kid?

LIN: Okay, I do remember that I loved being in
        the garden and watching the butterflies.

ALICE: Do you remember what your garden was like?

LIN: It was a small garden with a banyan tree
        that I climbed, and we had a rabbit hutch
        at the back. I was always busy with the
        rabbit and making sure the hutch was clean
        and cozy.

ALICE: You had a rabbit?

LIN: Yes.

ALICE: What kind of rabbit was it?

LIN: She was brown and fluffy. She was really
        small. A dwarf rabbit, tiny.

ALICE: Did she have a name?

LIN: Cookie.

ALICE: Good name. Tell me about Cookie . . .

LIN: She was so soft, like velvet. I loved
        stroking her and feeding her. I'm sure I
        wasn't supposed to give her so much food,
        but she didn't mind and I loved giving
        her treats. And she was always trying to
        escape.

ALICE: She sounds adorable. Were you the one who
        looked after her?

LIN: Yes, it was mostly me. Sometimes it was my
        sister, but she was more into petting her
        than looking after her. I cleaned out the
        hutch, fed her, filled the water bottle,
        and brushed her fur, although thinking
        back now I'm not sure she liked it much,
        but I loved brushing her. Sometimes I put
        her in my schoolbag and pretended to take
        her on little trips . . . actually she was
        probably my best friend.

ALICE: It sounds as though you really loved her,
        Lin, and looked after her so well. Can I
        just check in with how you're feeling as
        you're telling me about little Cookie?

LIN: Happy and sad at the same time . . . I
          guess as I'm thinking about her as my best
          friend, it makes me feel sad; it makes me
          remember how lonely I was.

ALICE: I get that. You felt really lonely, and you
          had a lot of love to give, which you gave
          to Cookie. And you did a great job looking
          after her; it was good that you had her.
          And I'm sorry you felt so alone. As you
          think about that memory now, petting and
          looking after Cookie, can you tell me a
          bit more about you, the little girl in the
          memory with her rabbit? What's she like?

LIN: She's really cute. I can see that she has
          her hair in bunches. She's actually really
          good at looking after Cookie, and has fun
          with her, she's resourceful, playful . . .
          and kind . . . [*Crying but smiling through
          the tears.*] She's happy playing with
          Cookie.

ALICE: I agree. She sounds really cute, and
          resourceful and kind and fun. Cookie was
          lucky to have her.

Lin

Fledgling belief: I'm alone, and no one will protect me.

Protective strategy: If I hide myself, don't let anyone else in, do well, and focus on others, then I'll be safe.

Unintended consequence: I'm cut off from myself, my needs, and my desires.

Flying belief: I'm cute, resourceful, playful, and kind.

* * *

*P*OSTSCRIPT: Thinking about a happy memory was what Lin needed to do to be able to see her younger self. It was only later that day that Lin told us she had been sexually abused by her uncle when she was five years old and that she thinks her mother had known about it. She had kept this memory hidden for so long, and it was so frightening to think about, that most of her memories from that time had also gone—blanked out to keep herself safe. That is how she survived the abuse growing up, but it was also why as an adult she felt lost. She hid who she was, scared of letting anyone get too close. She kept her focus on others, and did her very best in both her working life (as a radiologist) and in her relationship with her partner. But in the process, she lost herself. The route back for Lin was through connecting to a good memory, which enabled her to connect with herself as a kid. She knew who she was, even if it was hard for her to get there.

How about you? Were you able to get to your fledgling belief and strategies? How did you find going into a childhood memory? We'd invite you to make notes along the lines of your fellow guests to help you identify what sense you made of your early nest and how you've navigated your subsequent relationships. Have there been unintended consequences in adulthood from your childhood strategies?

CHAPTER 12

Scene IV

You're Precious

Cozy den. Early afternoon.

After lunch, ROBYN had felt so overwhelmed that she
had got in her car to leave, but at the driveway she
changed her mind and came back. She went to find RUTH
and told her why she had wanted to leave. The group
are now all gathered and ready to begin.

RUTH: Robyn has been feeling really overwhelmed,
       so much so that she almost left after
       lunch. But even though she's scared, she's
       here now and ready to share something with
       you all.

[ROBYN *stares at the ceiling, as if in another
world, or trying to escape this one, her leg
jiggling, she's clearly in distress; RUTH gently
asks if she's okay and if she needs anything; RUTH
goes to ROBYN, wraps a blanket round her shoulders,
and gives her a hug.*]

ROBYN: It was in my last year of elementary
       school. I was ten. My class got free
       swimming lessons for a term, and I was so
       excited because I'd never been to the local
       pool and always envied our neighbors who
       went every Saturday. Mum somehow managed to
       scrape together the money for my swimsuit,
       and I loved it-shiny red with crisscross
       straps at the back. It felt so grown-up.

I wore that swimsuit underneath my school
uniform every day before our first lesson.
The swimming coach told me I was a natural
but said that I needed goggles if I was
going to keep coming. I didn't want to tell
him the truth-that we couldn't afford them-
so I said I'd lost them. He told me not
to worry and that he'd bring a pair along
next time. He gave me a pair of brand-new
goggles at the start of our second lesson
and molested me in the changing rooms
afterward . . . I've never told anyone . . .
[*Looks down and covers her face in her
hands.*]

ALICE: Robyn, I'm so sorry to hear this happened
to you, and you must have been really
scared. It's not at all uncommon for
children not to tell anyone, because they
are frightened. I know this is not a place
you want to stay, and we won't stay any
longer than we have to. You are an adult
now, and it's not happening now, but let's
slow it down a little. See it as if it was
happening on a TV screen. Can you see the
little you? Do you remember how she felt?

ROBYN: I can.

ALICE: What is she feeling?

ROBYN: Scared.

ALICE: I'm sure she is; it was really scary. How
did she cope with feeling that scared?

ROBYN: She just kept it all to herself and tried to
forget.

ALICE: She was very resilient, and I'm thinking
that must have felt really lonely for
her . . .

ROBYN: She was so lonely. She just went into her
own little bubble and shut everyone out.

ALICE: Because there was no one she could trust.

ROBYN: No one. [*Face in hands as the tears finally
come.*]

ALICE: Stay with it for a little longer . . . with
all this going on, how was little Robyn
feeling about herself?

ROBYN: That she was all alone and no one cared.
That she was nothing.

ALICE: That must have been so hard . . . If you
keep her in mind for a moment longer, see
if you can step into the scene as the wise
adult you are now, reach out to her, and
take her by the hand. And now as you feel
that strength you have as an adult, take
her with you, out of the scene and somewhere
safe.

[*Pause.*]

Where do you take her?

ROBYN: To the small park near my house.

ALICE: And still holding her hand now, how is she
feeling there with you in the park?

ROBYN: Better . . . She's relieved. [*Sobbing.*]

ALICE: Good. She's got you now, she'll never be
alone again.

[*Pause.*]

Robyn, can you look at me for a moment? You've
just done a brave and kind thing, and whenever your
little self feels alone and scared, you can look
after her. You can take her hand and bring her

to the park where she can be with you while she's
upset, where she can feel safe.

ROBYN: That feels good actually, I can imagine
        that.

ALICE: And while you're imagining that, speaking
        to the part of her that feels as though
        she's nothing, what would you say?

ROBYN: I'm here. You're safe, you're precious.
[*Smiling through tears.*]

CHAPTER 13

Power and Shame

It is, and always has been, that those with power influence the identity of those without it and assign the rules
of engagement to which the less powerful must adhere.
This power dynamic is woven into the fabric of every family, institution, organization, culture, religion, and social
environment—and it is the overarching framework within
which we learn who we are. This hierarchy of power is the
backdrop to your heartbreak.

Fitting on that tiny glass slipper was the only thing standing between Cinderella and her happily-ever-after. The
"ugly" sisters' feet were on the larger side and—surprise,
surprise—the slipper didn't fit. Only the diminutive, perfect Cindy with those tiny, tiny toes could get the slipper

on and marry her prince. Throughout history, women have been rejected and shamed for having bodies—or feet—that don't fit the cultural prescription of beauty. The idea of the diminutive equating to feminine attractiveness is as pervasive as it is shaming. Your feet are just your feet. The value system telling you how your feet are supposed to look is what creates the shame.

The stories about who women are and where they rank go back a long, long way. The story of Adam and Eve is often called the story of original sin and—surprise, surprise—it was Eve's fault. Weak Eve (for being tempted by the serpent). Wicked Eve (for being hungry). Fast-forward a few thousand years and we're being burned as witches (a wart on the face was enough), discarded at birth for not being male (no vaginas here, thanks), shamed for menstruating (standard), and mutilated lest we have sexual pleasure (no words). This global historical and cultural context situates and infuses the experience of women—before we're even born.

The psychological fallout from all this is pervasive and painful and attacks the very core of your self-worth with a narrative that whispers, *You are worthless,* and *Shame be upon you.* With disempowerment comes invalidation, and sadly this is the plight of women all over the world.

Controlling the conversation, trivializing, dismissing, punishing, ignoring, humiliating, shaming, denying, manipulating–these are the mechanisms through which power *can* be exercised. It sounds a bit like this:

You're not thinking clearly.

You know you sound insane right now.

You're making a big deal out of nothing, as always.

You can't take a joke.

You take everything so personally.

You're being oversensitive.

You're overthinking this.

It's your fault, not mine.

I never said that.

You're the problem here, not me.

I haven't got time for this.

I'm doing this because I love you.

Why would you think that?

This says more about you than me.

It's your fault I cheated; you're not hot enough.

It didn't happen like that.

You're making it up.

You're irrational.

You're wrong.

You're always getting it muddled.

What's the matter with you?

You need therapy.

Are you really going to wear that?

You used to be fun.

It's not important.

It doesn't matter.

It didn't happen.

And to minimize the threat posed by such gaslighting, the following strategies are often employed to manage it: self-surveillance, self-blame, deference, self-silencing, tolerance of "misbehavior," appeasement, compliance, withdrawal, body hating, overeating, undereating, ruminating, self-harm, self-criticism, and self-punishment. It looks like this:

If you lost weight, they might give you the
time of day, and be sure to think twice before
you speak up in case it provokes them.

Be totally cool with the odd affair.

Don't complain if they don't empty the dishwasher—
they've had a hard day, after all—and tell them
they look wonderful so they don't hit you.

Ruminate on how to do better and be sure to buy the
latest self-help book and brutalize your body at the gym.

Look over your shoulder, stay safe.

Cry if you must (but only into your pillow,
lest you disturb their sleep).

Drink gallons of wine, and with any luck, you'll forget.

Don't tell anyone they're treating you badly ... because
it's all your fault.

Back down or go down.

Put out or shut up.

Sympathize and empathize with all their problems and
make excuses for them ... because it's not easy being
them.

None of us would really give this advice, nor do we set out to be in relationships where we operate like this, yet we can all see ourselves reflected somewhere here. This is what happens when you're on the losing side of the power dynamic. And it is these everyday micro-betrayals that magnify your heartbreak, the ongoing accumulation of which adds up to extreme frustration, diminished agency, shame, and negative self-worth (*hwa-byung*, even).

This toxic mix is felt in the body—heat in the cheeks, stirring in the stomach, dry mouth, eyes downcast, posture sinking, nausea. Your body is always the first responder, tightening around shame and invalidation, colluding to keep it secret. You retreat inside yourself, and time slows down as you try to disconnect and hide from what's happening, willing it all to go away. And in this hidden place, the shame can attach to your early fledgling beliefs like a limpet.

But the truth is that none of this has got anything to do with who you are and has everything to do with the definitions that those in power give you in order to maintain the status quo. They were never your definitions in the first place. Not when you were a child and not now as an adult. They belong to those who have sought to control you.

When you are rejected or replaced or cheated on, when the person you love and trust chooses someone else over you, the shame is on them. And if your heartbreaker tries to manipulate you into believing it's the other way around (*you're not seeing it from my perspective; you never stick up for me; you're always making me feel small; you never cared about what I needed; you don't value my opinion; you love the kids more than me and always put them first*), don't take it on. Their shame is not yours to feel—it belongs to them.

Shame will tell you to bury all the evidence lest you expose the faults that lie deep within you (or your feet). And this creates problems: it's lonely keeping secrets, it disconnects you from others, and it takes energy to keep them suppressed. So, let's turn it around, connect with others, and start sharing our "shameful" secrets. Ruth and I find it very bonding to share the fact that we both have large feet and to laugh about the ways they have defined us. How has the shape and size of your feet (or any other body part) shaped how you think about yourself as a woman? #bigfeetarebeautifultoo.

Social and physical shaming is a mechanism used by those in power to discredit entire groups of people on account of their gender, race, sexual orientation, education, religion, language, income, immigration status, ability. *Shame be upon you* for your being different than those in power.

Women can be diminished in many underhand and subtle ways, which gradually become internalized–*drip, drip, drip*–until what you have been told about yourself becomes indistinguishable from who you think you are.

You're a bit of a show-off.
#justexpressingmyself

Are you on your period?
#beingawoman

You asked for it.
#metoo

You're boring.
#imtired

You're always tired.
#fightingthepatriarchyisexhausting

One of the hardest kinds of subordination to spot is the backhanded compliment–flattering yet simultaneously invalidating. It's subordination disguised as sweet talk, an unpleasant sting that can be tricky to pin down.[1]

You look so great in that photo; I didn't recognize you at first.
(Inference: You usually look rough.)

I wish I could be so relaxed about all this clutter.
(Inference: You're a slob.)

You scrub up well.
(Inference: You look like shit most of the time.)

Ooh, you look so comfy in that outfit.
(Inference: I wouldn't be seen dead in it.)

I wish I had as much time on my hands as you do.
(Inference: You're lazy.)

Your house is so cozy.
(Inference: You're poor and have no style.)

You're coping so much better than I thought you would.
(Inference: You're usually on the verge of a nervous breakdown.)

Your hair looks good today.
(Inference: It's a bird's nest most of the time.)

When we adopt the lens of those who seek to disempower and weaken us, it not only brings *us* down; it brings *all women* down. Recognizing these messages for what they are—instruments of invalidation—is the first step toward breaking free of them. These barbed insults in disguise are designed to keep you in your place. They are not the truth.

We know that shame can be hard to spot. It's often present just outside of view when you're feeling terrible about yourself, when you want to avoid or withdraw from others, when you are ruminating on your mistakes, when you're feeling fearful of rejection or being found out, when you are feeling exhausted and defeated, and reaching for the wine. Bring your shameful secrets out into the light by telling someone you trust. Write them down and burn the paper. Take whatever steps you need to rid yourself of them. Let your feet be your feet… and be proud.

Have a think back to the work you did on your childhood self. Is the shame you feel now connected to your early nest experience and your fledgling beliefs? Chances are the shame you are feeling may be linked to early life experiences. Perhaps it was a parent, teacher, school bully, sibling, first love, or religious leader who invalidated you, and if so, it's important you leave it with them.

PART III

The Future

CHAPTER 14

Handing It Back

The wider world around you will always have a view about what you should be doing, what or who you should want, what success looks like, and what you *really* need. Some of it may be worth listening to, but a lot of it isn't. The clamor of competing voices directs our wants and desires every time we switch on our phones. The algorithms in the ether push and pull us this way and that, promising us happiness and fulfillment if only we buy their latest gadget, drink their Kool-Aid, pop their pill, join their club, and follow them, because, well... everyone else is doing it.

Heartbreak changes futures, often obliterating them. Your plans, dreams, certainties, and hopes may have altered radically and left you with a sense of swirling uncertainty and groundlessness. We get that. But we are now moving into a different space, in which you will reimagine your future and return once more to what you really love and want. We're not going to approach this by looking at things in a linear fashion. There's nothing more daunting than seeing a vast expanse of time stretching before you and thinking you have to make a plan for it right away. Instead, we're going to focus only on now—the present. Each decision you make in the present moment creates a future.

Futures unfold—they don't already exist.

*　　*　　*

We are going to take you through an exercise now that will set the intention for and context in which you will start to rethink who you are. We've been into the past and dismantled some of the scaffolding of your early thoughts and behaviors, and now we need to clear some space for something new and purposeful to emerge.

Okay. Find a comfortable position, sit back, and relax. The first part is a meditation. We'd invite you to read it through a few times before closing your eyes and imagining it.

Take a deep breath and feel the tension leave your body as you settle into a place of self-reflection and healing.

Take another deep breath and another, and be aware that with each breath you take, you become more deeply relaxed and at ease.

Feel yourself drifting, peaceful and relaxed, deeper and deeper into a comfortable place within yourself.

You can feel yourself becoming more relaxed now with each new breath.

Your body is breathing a sigh of relief, as you just let go and settle into a deeper sense of ease and comfort.

Your mind and heart are becoming free from worry, and a warm, peaceful sensation is spreading within your chest.

You can feel your entire body breathing a sigh of comfort and relief, as you drift further and further into a deep, soothing peace. Just allow any tension you find to be there, and feel it slowly drifting away.

Now imagine a circle of warm, soft light at the top of your head.

Slowly feel that circle expand to spread across your head and face, soothing and caressing your skin as it gently relaxes all the muscles in your face and forehead.

Feel the warm waves of relaxation continuing to drift easily and naturally down into your neck, then quietly spreading across your shoulders.

Notice the tension leaving your body as you take another deep, cleansing breath.

The mild, comforting waves of relaxation are spreading down your arms and across your chest now, washing away any distress, tension, or discomfort that was there.

Your entire torso is feeling more comfortable and relaxed now, as the waves of comfort and ease spread farther down your body.

Your hips and stomach are feeling the relaxation spread and wash through them, bringing soothing comfort naturally and easily into your upper legs and thighs.

As this feeling of letting go continues, notice how it slowly spreads across and around your knees, your lower legs, and your calves.

Now the warm waves of relaxation are reaching your feet, and you notice how all the tension that was in your upper body is leaving through your toes, giving you a general sense of quiet, calm, and ease.

Now imagine that you are seeing yourself at a much, much younger age, somewhere before the age of ten years old.

You are totally safe and in charge as you travel back to see your younger self again.

We'd like you to imagine her outside, somewhere by

the sea perhaps, or on a mountain or in a park or wood-
land, and picture the scene around you. What can you
see? What can you smell? What can you hear? In your
mind's eye you see that the little girl that is you is wearing
a sweater over her clothes—it can be any color you like—
and on that sweater, you can see that something has been
written. When you look closely, you see that it is the fledgling belief you were given about yourself.

Now, gently and lovingly, we want you to ask your
younger self to remove the sweater and hand it over to
you.

In the distance, you both see the person who gave her
the fledgling belief, and on her behalf you approach this
person and give them the sweater; you hand back the
fledgling belief that was not yours to have.

As you do, gently say to this person, "I forgive you. I'm
sorry for your pain," and invite them to hand the sweater
back to whoever it was that gave it to them.

In this way, the belief gets handed back across the generations.

Now turn back to your younger self. She's been patiently
waiting and watching.

As you lovingly approach her, you hand her a new

sweater and ask her to put it on. You can help her if you'd like.

Once she has it on, you both see that the sweater has something written on it—the new, updated flying belief that you created for your little self.

Read it, savor the way it sounds, the way it makes you feel to give her this flying belief, and notice the expression on her face as she takes it in.

Give her a big hug now and tell her, "You are loved. You are seen. You are understood."

Spend as much time as you'd like in this hug; feel how good it is to be in contact with her. Tell her that you will always protect her, always care for her, and always give her what she needs. She doesn't even have to ask.

We'd like you to focus on your breath again now and become gently aware of the sounds around you and the present moment. And when you are ready, give yourself a nod of acknowledgment that you have had this experience and taken part in something deeply compassionate that is larger than yourself, and in so doing contributed to healing the heartbreaking ancestral echoes that extend far beyond your own heartbreak.

CHAPTER 15

Emotional Regulation

Whatever you are feeling right now is okay. Let it be. You will come to see that you need all your feelings; they are signals from your body that help you orientate and understand what's needed.

Feelings have a shared trajectory. They peak and trough, ebb and flow, come and go. Some stay around for longer, others are brief—but like the tides, they have a natural pulsation, in and out. What they don't do is intensify forever. Still, when those difficult ones do intensify, you might find yourself wanting to short-circuit them. A glass of wine (or a bottle), the Instagram-a-thon, a sugar-induced sofa coma— we've all been there. And getting away from feelings does create short-term relief. But in the long term, burying, avoiding, or cutting off from them will lead you to believe that they're unmanageable and frightening and leave you bereft of the vital information they contain. So have them and let them do their job—which is to guide you.

You need all your feelings, even the ones you don't like. They are important and necessary and serve a purpose. If you feel angry, there has been an injustice. If you feel afraid, that signals danger. And if you feel calm, there is safety and connection.

Your feelings are your internal barometer telling you when you need to act and when you don't. We have three emotional systems that work together to guide us: Defend, Drive, and Recover.[1] Each is important and necessary, and it is through the three working together in a balanced way that emotional equilibrium is reached and maintained.

Defend   Drive   Recover

Defend is our red zone, flashing to alert us to danger. To keep ourselves safe, this system uses powerful feelings such as anger, fear, and disgust to charge our bodies with cortisol and adrenaline hormones so that we can protect ourselves from danger. But there are many other feelings that can also make us feel under threat. Here are some of them:

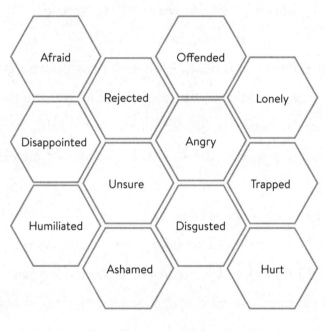

Defend Emotions

Programmed over millennia, Defense is the most dominant of our three systems and is extremely sensitive to threat from both the external landscape (lions, heartbreakers, muggers), and the internal one (images, thoughts, and memories). It's like having your own sentry guard on permanent watch, alerting you whenever something seems wrong—physically, morally, or emotionally—and triggering your survival responses: fight, flight, freeze, or fawn.

Think of a cat-and-mouse chase. The tiny mouse first tries to outrun the quick-witted cat, scampering about at breakneck speed, its defense system in overdrive—this *flee* response is the mouse's superskill. After all, it's not going to come out well from a *fight* against this feline enemy, so on it runs, under, over, this way and that. But the cat just keeps on coming at it, paw after paw, pounce after pounce, and before long the mouse is going to be completely exhausted. But the little mouse has one final option, the last resort, and it's a very clever one. It goes completely limp, mentally checks out, and feigns death—if it's going to be eaten, it may as well be unconscious when it happens. The mouse *freezes*. Confused by this sudden turn of events, the cat paws at its immobile body, willing it to move so the chase can start up again—it's the chase the cat loves (mean, isn't it?)—but to no avail. Kitty eventually gets bored and wanders off in search of a livelier victim to taunt, at which point the mouse "comes to" and makes good its escape.

Like the mouse, you too have all these responses. But unlike the mouse, you have an extra superpower—the ability to make friends with the enemy. You can read the social and emotional cues in a dangerous situation and, unlike mice, use your relational knowledge to talk your way out. You can cast your eyes to the ground, flatter, apologize, agree, and in any number of ways make yourself unobjectionable and nonthreatening to mitigate danger and enact a *fawn* response. If only the mouse knew a joke or two.

Drive, the blue zone, propels us toward achieving what we want and need. Associated with feelings of excitement, purpose, and agency, it's our pleasure and prosper mechanism, alerting us to what's possible and giving us the energy to achieve it. This is where our energy and hope lie, where we feel most alive. Drive is fulfilled when what you're doing is aligned with what you want, knowing all the while that Defend is available when you need it. When this system is guiding us, our body is flooded with dopamine and we feel happy, motivated, alert, and focused.

Recover, the green zone, is all about feeling warm, peaceful, and contented. It has a safe and unworried vibe—a cocoon of connection. Oxytocin and endorphins flood our bodies as we rest and recharge the batteries, leaving us feeling soothed and ready for anything. When Defend and Drive are guiding us, our bodies are charged

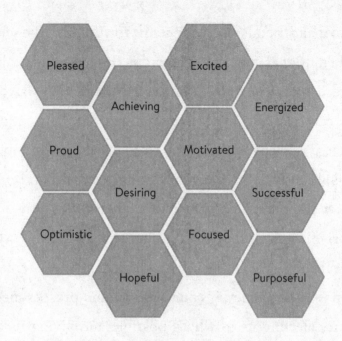

Drive Emotions

and active, but when we are in Recovery mode, our bodies are able to digest all those active hormones and return to a more peaceful, calm, and settled state of being.

We need to feel safe to sink into the green zone. No one can set about resting and recovering while there is danger. For all animals, us included, physical and emotional safety is a prerequisite for us to let down our guard, discharge all those high-energy hormones, and replenish our emotional and physical tanks. The fullest expression of the green zone is when we are in connection with others, feeling accepted, supported, and loved. Self-help is good, but together-help is even better.

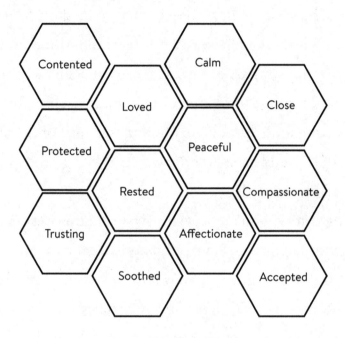

Recovery Emotions

If the Heartbreak Hotel was a color, it would be green.

It is our green system that we often give the least attention to. In our high-pressured, fast-paced, striving culture, we rarely give ourselves permission to be in green. So let's help each other get there. We'll put money on your being better at *greening* for others than you are for yourself, so you definitely know how. And if someone wants to help you, keep in mind the pleasure you feel when someone asks *you* for help and offer them that same experience in return. Because when someone offers to be there for you, they are *greening* for you. It is a communication of care and kindness, an act of love. If you're someone who worries about being a burden on others, think of it like this—by not asking for help, you are robbing someone of the pleasure they would have experienced from being needed and valued by you.

Heartbreak is an emotionally dysregulating experience of great magnitude. Your red map is flashing neon with fear and anger, green is nowhere to be seen, and blue has been thrown overboard by your heartbreaker. You're struggling to find *any* green, unable to sleep, let alone rest—and we understand this. But no amount of trying to motivate yourself out of your feelings, or propel yourself onward before you are ready, is going to get you to where you want to go. Take a rest instead ... a short rest will leave you much stronger physically and emotionally than any amount of screen time ... or wine.

Most people still find this difficult despite feeling completely exhausted. While relaxation can take many forms— running, meditation, yoga, or hanging out with friends, for example–green is best when it's a low-stimulation activity, something peaceful and quiet. The brain and body need downtime, so avoid anything that will put you back into a Drive mode. Screens may be relaxing, but they do not qualify as rest. And rest is never lazy; it is a necessary prerequisite for you to gather your strength. Think of it as an investment in your future. And if the idea of silence makes you nervous, try gentle music in its place. If you are struggling to sleep, know that the simple act of being quiet and keeping still in a dark room is restorative.

If you're currently feeling masses of red, worrying about your feelings overwhelming you, or feeling completely overwrought with the whole business of your heartbreak, here are a few more techniques you can use to help bring the temperature down and enable you to think more clearly.

Balloon Breathing

Place your hand on your belly.

Imagine that your belly is a balloon.

Take a deep breath and fill that balloon with air.

Then, exhaling slowly, deflate the balloon.

*Now close your eyes and really feel that balloon
inflating and deflating as you continue to breathe.*

*As you feel more and more relaxed—and when you're ready—
breathe out and let the balloon slowly drift away into the sky.*

The Butterfly Hug

*Cross your hands over your chest, palms
facing inward, and link your thumbs.*[2]

Make sure your middle fingers are resting lightly on your collarbone.

Raise your elbows to create your butterfly wings.

Slowly tap your hands on your chest, alternating left and right.

*While tapping, breathe in through your nose and
out through your mouth until you feel calm.*

What sits behind the butterfly hug, and the reason it's so effective, is the principle of bilateral stimulation. It turns out there is a kind of magic to be found in the simple rhythmic movements of our bodies. And it's not limited to the butterfly hug. Jogging, walking, banging the drums, anything that involves alternating movements can qualify.

This was discovered by chance by psychologist Francine Shapiro, during a walk in a park. She noticed that some distressing feelings she was having suddenly stopped. She realized that walking while she was thinking about them helped her to feel better, beyond the expected benefits of the fresh air and aerobic exercise. Bilateral stimulation activates both sides of the brain, allowing it to better process information, something your brain does naturally during REM sleep, which can help distressing memories settle down.

You may have built bilateral stimulation into your daily life in ways you're unaware of. When you alternate taps on the steering wheel or tap your arms or legs to music and find yourself somehow soothed; when you decide to go for a walk to "clear your head"; it's the bilateral stimulation that does it. Utilize the restorative power of bilateral stimulation, and let your body do the processing for you in any way you like. Practice getting into green through your body—and your mind will follow.

CHAPTER 16

The Compass

What matters to you? What do you want and need? It may have been a very long time since you last asked yourself this, especially if you have spent many years in service to others.

Let's take that time now.

Values are not concrete. They are more like important principles through which you can articulate your next steps. They are not the same as goals, which usually have an end point. Values are your direction of travel. Values endure; they cannot be completed or achieved. They are ways of living—ideals, if you like—characterized by fullness, purpose, and vital engagement. Think of them as foundations shoring up a home: the home will always be steady if it's built on solid ground. Any goals you create for yourself in the future will be infused by your values—like a drop of lemon in a glass of water.

Let's first deal with the imperatives of *should*, *must*, and *ought*. They are commanding and authoritative, ordering you around in an aggressive and often tyrannical way. We use them to get ourselves or others to do things we don't want to do. We'd like you to consider these imperatives very lightly as we go on, preferably bracketing them off completely. Imperatives are usually coming from other people's expectations of you, and they may not be in your best interests.

In their place, we want your own needs and desires to come into play. Less of the imperative and more of the inquisitive.

Remember we said we'd never ask you to do something we hadn't done ourselves? Well, it was identifying our own values that led us here, to you…

ALICE. After my mother died, I was thrown into a disorientated, lost state of feeling, like being a child again. I'd spent almost a decade looking after my mum, alongside bringing up young children, teaching, and running a private practice. It occurred to me in the first few weeks of grief that over the previous decade I had gone from someone who felt I knew who I was and what made me tick, to being completely at a loss. It was all a big mess in my head, with no clear way through. I was on compassionate leave from my various professional roles but couldn't find any energy or forward motion.

So I did what I had asked many, many of my clients to do in their times of disorientation: I did a values clarification exercise. And in doing it, I realized this: I needed to laugh more and have more joy in my life. I wanted to honor the introvert that I am with more solitude and quietness. I needed to reconsider the relationships in my life and nurture the connections that were nourishing for me. And I wanted more abundance and fullness in my life and to keep learning.

Nearly three years on, I am happier, more fulfilled. Not because I set out to be, but because the grief showed me that I needed to get back to myself, and because, through making decisions aligned with my values, I now have a more joyful, meaningful, and connected life. The consequence of ignoring what mattered to me had pretty much led me to burnout and exhaustion. Looking back at that period now, the period before my mum died, I had come very far from myself and was suffering as a result. Grief and the disorientation it brought were the catalyst to get back together with myself.

RUTH. Alice was convinced of the transformative value of this exercise, something she had recently done. She was passionate about it and I was intrigued because she seemed different—more energized and purposeful—and I wanted a piece of the action! It wasn't easy, but I did it.

What came up for me was how much I wanted to help others. I had been writing a novel, but the prospect of finding an audience for it was getting slimmer. I enjoyed writing very much, but I wasn't sure I was being driven by what was really important to me. I wrote down my values in the front of my journal to help keep me focused and oriented toward what I decided mattered to me most: compassion, connection, commitment, grace.

Having them close always keeps me moving in the right direction, and as it turned out, within a very short space of time I was back in my happy place writing a book—this time, one driven by my values. There is no doubt in my mind that I am where I am right now, writing down these words, because I took the time to do this work.

*   *   *

As we go through this exercise together, remember that no one else ever needs to know your values unless you choose to tell them. You never need to explain or justify what is important to you—that it makes sense to *you* is all that matters. Engage with this exercise as if nobody is watching. Dance while you're at it if you'd like. Having other people whispering their judgments and imperatives over your shoulder is not helpful at this stage (or any stage, actually). We want you to have the freedom and space to really connect back with yourself.

We hope that this feels like an exciting idea for you, but it may also feel scary. That's okay. Making new choices requires that you act in the face of fear, not in the absence of it.

You may find that what matters most to you now connects all the way back to what has always mattered to you, but which has been obscured over the years by the many demands of life. Before we go on, cast your mind back to your childhood. What did you like doing then? What was important to you? If as a kid you really loved animals, you don't now have to retrain as a vet (although you could!), but having an animal in your life might be nourishing and important for you.

ALICE. When I was at school, I wanted to become an artist. It was a happy and creative place for me, where my introversion could roam free and I could express myself without an audience. But I was given career advice by my school and told that artists don't earn a living—and anyway, it wouldn't get me into a good university (no one thought to suggest art school...)—so I dropped art in favor of something more "academic."

The values of "success," "academic achievement," and "education" infused—even commanded—that decision, and while they may not be my values *now*, I can radically accept that I was guided by them *then*. And it led me to a career in psychology, so no great harm. And art lingers on somewhere on the periphery, occasionally coming into view and giving me happy hours of creation.

*   *   *

Can you think of an equivalent? Families hold quite strong values, as do wider cultures. Girls not being educated well (or at all), for example, financial security, faith, independence—see if you can link your "inherited" values to any of the big (and small) choices you have made.

Try to be honest with yourself. Notice how you judge what may or may not be important to you. Perhaps you feel embarrassed by one of your values, wishing it was something else instead. Don't listen to or trust these judgments, not for now, and maybe not ever. Hold them lightly, turn them down, mute them, bracket them. Whatever works.

Breaking Free

An espalier is a frame used to train fruit trees to grow in a two-dimensional shape. Flat up against a wall or fence, their branches are forced to grow horizontally rather than up and out. But did anyone ask the tree what he, she, or they thought? Despite such crippling restrictions, the tree still grows on to fulfill its new destiny, but perhaps not the one it might have chosen for itself. Let's remove the shackles. Your next chapter will be shaped *by* you *for* you.

To help you connect to your values, here is a big list of possibilities. Read them through and notice which ones you resonate with. As you go through the list, try not to think too hard or dwell too long on anything at this stage;

just note which ones chime. The list is not exhaustive. If you think of a value that's not on there, that's great too—add it on and choose it if you want. And don't worry about how many you go for. Some people will choose a few and others nearly all of them! There is no right or wrong (that would be a judgment).

Abundance—to appreciate and invite in the fullness of life

Acceptance—to be open and accepting

Accountability—to own my actions

Achievement—to fulfill my goals

Adventure—to create, explore, and seek novelty and stimulation

Advocacy—to speak up on behalf of others

Assertiveness—to respectfully stand up for my rights and needs

Authenticity—to be genuine and real, and true to myself

Beauty—to cultivate, create, and nurture beauty in myself and all around me

Care—to look after myself and others

Challenge—to challenge myself to grow, learn, and improve

Charity—to give and not to count the cost

Commitment—to follow through on my intentions

Compassion—to seek to understand and be kind

Connection—to foster relationships and community

Contribution—to make a positive difference

Cooperation—to cooperate and collaborate with others

Courage—to persist in the face of fear

Creativity—to be innovative and expressive

Fairness—to treat people without discrimination

Fitness—to look after my physical and mental health

Flexibility—to adjust and adapt to changing circumstances

Forgiveness—to be forgiving toward myself and others

Freedom—to choose with autonomy and self-determination

Friendliness—to be friendly, companionable, and agreeable

Fun—to seek out opportunities for fun

Generosity—to be generous, sharing, and giving of myself

Grace—to act with dignity

Gratitude—to be grateful and appreciative

Honesty—to be truthful and open in all that I do

Hope—to believe in possibility

Humor–to find the funny

Industry–to be dedicated to the work I choose

Integrity–to honor my word

Joy–to delight in and be delighted by life

Kindness–to be considerate and nurturing

Love–to act lovingly and affectionately

Mindfulness–to be present to my experience

Open-mindedness–to be open to new ideas and perspectives

Organization–to be orderly and efficient

Passion–to find and pursue what excites me

Peace–to be still and free from conflict

Power–to have confidence and influence over my life

Safety–to protect from physical or emotional harm

Self-control–to act with good judgment

Sensuality–to explore and enjoy my body

Skillfulness–to practice and improve my skills

Spirituality–to connect with something bigger than myself

Trust–to be honest and transparent

Once you have your list of values, the next step is to make them workable by grouping them together with others that are similar. For example, kindness and compassion might be in the same group. Take time with this, and it can be revisited as many times as you'd like over the coming days, weeks, and months. For now, see if you can organize your values according to likeness into *four* groups.

Once you have your four groups, pick the value from each that best captures the spirit of the collective—one value word that will speak on behalf of all the others. And once you have, also write in large letters the meaning attached to it.

We hope that these values are starting to set your heart alight, just a little bit. They represent your new path ahead.

Imagine that you are on a boat in the Pacific, far out from the nearest landmass, with icy Alaska to the north and the warmer climes of Mexico to the east. You're longing to be on the beach, sipping mango juice and watching the sun set. You can't see land right now, and you need to set the direction of travel—because you don't want to expend energy traveling toward the icy poles when you are hoping to reach warmer climes. Think of your values as your internal GPS, guiding you toward what is important to you even when storms rage, winds try to throw you off course, and you can't see a damn thing.

Okay, let's put your GPS to the test.

Think now about a decision that you need to make in the coming days. It could be something quite ordinary, like whether or not you're going to go out tonight, or it could be one of those bigger life decisions, such as whether to move house or change a relationship. Bring the upcoming decision to mind and note down all the possible choices you could make in relation to it.

With your GPS to hand, ask yourself this:

> *Which of these possible choices is most*
> *in service to my values?*

The one that most aligns is the one that will take you toward yourself.

Let's say you are trying to work everything out and keep coming back to "I still love them." Round and round you go. They have betrayed you, but you still love them— it's an impossible merry-go-round of a dialectic. *I love them and want to be with them, and I want to leave them.*

Now let's bring your values into focus and see whether they can help orientate your next choices. Let's say they look like this:

Integrity—to honor my word

Freedom—to choose with autonomy and self-determination

Grace—to act with dignity

Joy—to delight in and be delighted by life

Which direction will take you toward a future aligned with what is important and meaningful to you and one that is led by freedom, grace, integrity, or joy? If your values seem to contradict each other—for example, compassion takes you back to the one who's betrayed you, but freedom takes you in the other direction—be curious about that. It's a dialectic. Hold the tension; you can be both compassionate toward your betrayer and leave them. There will be times when you have to make decisions that take you off course—that's life—but overall, the weight of balance needs to be in favor of your values. It is through routinely asking yourself this question—*Is the decision I'm about to make in service to my values?*—that you'll create a future path aligned with what is most important to you.

Choice Points

In any given situation we have a choice . . . we can move toward what matters to us or away from it.

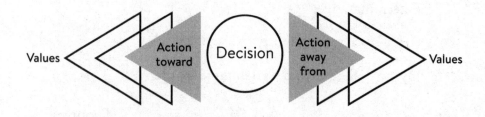

Values — Action toward — Decision — Action away from — Values

Is the decision I'm about to make in service to my values?

Think of one action you could take today that would be fully aligned with one of your values. What is it?

Do it.

Choosing and deciding in this way is how you accumulate a meaningful and purposeful ongoing future. And you don't even have to ask yourself the question *What am I going to do with my future?* because your future is simply unfolding before your eyes with every single values-aligned decision you make.

When faced with a choice, you will find yourself pulled back in the direction of your old belief system, and this will take a while to change. The first thing to do when this happens is to take a moment to notice that you are doing it. Ask yourself, *Am I using my fledgling belief to make this decision, or my flying belief?* Choose in the direction of your flying belief and your values, even if it feels a bit unusual, uncomfortable, or peculiar. It won't feel this way for long.

Notice who in your life encourages you toward your values, who helps make effortless the manifestation of what matters to you—and notice who doesn't. If you find that your new values take you anywhere near a Dark Triad type, listen to your key people, remember the work you've done so far, and let them help steer you back on course.

The Rickety Train

Imagine you are planning to take a train heading somewhere special that you've been longing to visit.[1]

You stand on the station platform, waiting for the train to arrive.

Two trains pull in, and you see that both are headed for your chosen destination.

One of them appears to be a bit dirty, shabby even, and you can see that some of the seats are worn and frayed. It looks odd, unfamiliar, and uncomfortable.

The other one looks much safer: it's clean and the seats look really comfy and plush; it has free Wi-Fi, air-conditioning, and a fancy dining car.

It feels risky to opt for the rickety train, so you hop aboard the safer-looking one and get settled.

Meanwhile, the rickety train pulls out of the station and makes its way toward your chosen destination. As you wait patiently, you see another pull out and then another.

Still, you think it will be well worth the wait as surely the comfy train will leave soon.

But what if it never leaves the station?

What if the rickety train, despite looking shabby and uncomfortable, is the only way to get to where you want to go?

Sometimes we get stuck in familiar grooves and turn away from the discomfort of the unknown, waiting for things to get better.

But here's the thing: If you keep making the same choices, the same thing will keep happening. New choices do create discomfort, but they might just take you where you're longing to get to.

CHAPTER 17

New Perspectives

What do you see when you look at this picture?

Can you see the duck? And the rabbit? Over the previous pages you have created a new perspective on who you are, but that doesn't mean you will automatically lose sight of how you saw yourself before. As you move forward, expect some interplay, some movement back-

and-forth between the different viewpoints—it's all part of the process of living into freedom. Much like this optical illusion, where one picture can be seen in two ways, you can practice moving between views of yourself. By being able to see both perspectives, you'll expand your view of yourself *and* your future.

Think of an elephant, a huge, fully grown elephant that has been tamed and put to work clearing forests. When it's not working, it is tied up with an insubstantial chain attached to a peg in the ground to prevent its escape. With one stamp of its foot, the elephant could break free. But it doesn't. When it was young, it was tied up with the exact same chain, but it wasn't big or strong enough to break it. As it grew, the imprint of that early experience endured, and even though as a grown adult one tug of its now mighty leg would be enough to break free—the elephant doesn't know this. The early lesson prevails, and the elephant's captivity is ensured. If only it knew . . .

The grown-up elephant doesn't know how to live freely, but you do.

Freedom is created the moment you realize you are not bound by your early beliefs and that you can make different choices as an adult from the perspective of your flying beliefs. Living into that reality can feel both exhilarating and frightening.

There will be moments of uncertainty, even moments where you long for the familiarity and routine of your previous life, but if you just keep going, you will eventually see the full picture of your many possibilities.

When Irene was groomed by her betrayer for money, she blamed herself. She *knew* it was all her fault because, just like when she was young, she hadn't been careful and should have seen it coming. And so she resolved again to be more careful. But armed with a new belief, she was able to have her elephant-stamping-its-foot moment. Her adult self told her young self that she was capable and full of fun and passion and that she can trust herself. This was the pivotal moment for Irene. She saw the truth of it—her brother's accident wasn't her fault, and nor was the betrayal.

This was the new possibility she created:

Irene

New perspective: I am capable and full of fun and passion. I can trust myself.

Values:

Adventure—to create, explore, and seek novelty and stimulation

Kindness—to be considerate and nurturing

Fun—to seek out opportunities for fun

Contribution—to make a positive difference

Nadia's perspective shifted from holding a fledgling belief: *I'm stupid and disappointing;* to a new flying belief: *I am smart, and I have a voice.* Once she realized that the strategy born of her fledgling belief hadn't spared her from being betrayed, she saw that she no longer needed to hide away by asking so many questions and created a new perspective.

This was the new possibility she created:

Nadia

New perspective: I am smart, and I have a voice.

Values:

Industry—to be dedicated to the work I choose

Passion—to find and pursue what excites me

Abundance—to appreciate and invite in the fullness of life

Courage—to persist in the face of fear

Eshe's perspective shifted from a fledgling belief: *I'm no good, and it's my fault that bad things happen,* created when she fell and cut herself at her parents' barbeque; to a flying belief: *I'm lovable. It's not my fault. I'm important and can ask for help.* And with this shift, she no longer needed to keep everyone safe and put others first. And her own needs came into view.

This was the new possibility she created:

Eshe

New perspective: I'm lovable. It's not my fault. I'm important and can ask for help.

Values:

Sensuality—to explore and enjoy my body

Compassion—to seek to understand and be kind

Fairness—to treat people without discrimination

Mindfulness—to be present to my experience

Lin's perspective shifted from a fledgling belief: *I'm alone, and no one will protect me;* to believing she possessed many new qualities to which she had previously been oblivious. When this came into view, she realized she could drop her old *win all the prizes* strategy and just be herself. Her new perspective was that she was *cute, resourceful, playful, and kind.*

This was the new possibility she created:

Lin

New perspective: I'm cute, resourceful, playful, and kind.

Values:

Accountability—to own my actions

Beauty—to cultivate, create, and nurture beauty in myself and all around me

Creativity—to be innovative and expressive

Freedom—to choose with autonomy and self-determination

Robyn saw that, far from being *alone* and *bad,* she did matter and her feelings did count. With this, she created and updated a new perspective that she was not only *brave* and *good,* but she was also *precious* and *can be safe with others.* Instead of disconnecting to protect herself, she could connect with those around her.

This was the new possibility she created:

Robyn

New perspective: I'm precious, and I can be safe with others.

Values:

Connection—to foster relationships and community

Joy—to delight in and be delighted by life

Fitness—to look after my physical and mental health

Integrity—to honor my word

What is your new perspective? Bring to mind how your younger self felt in your memory and how your adult self shifted that formative view. If you really believed that new perspective, if you really lived into your values, what might be possible for you now?

If you find yourself slipping back toward your fledgling beliefs and old protective strategies, don't judge yourself; notice it's happening, be understanding and empathetic toward yourself, and switch channels. Compassion is the antidote to judgment. You have worn the old coat for such a long time, it's no wonder it's comfy and familiar. As you try on this new coat, woven from your flying belief, it's going to take some getting used to. But trust us: once you've worn it in, this new coat will become your firm favorite.

How does that feel? Sit with it for a bit...

If you now find that your old thoughts are flooding back, don't tell yourself not to think them. Instead, try this and then change channels.

Floating Leaves

Imagine it's a warm sunny day and you are sitting by a gentle meandering stream shaded by large oak trees.[1] The clear water flows over smooth rocks and pebbles as it descends through a peaceful valley.

Every so often, a big leaf drops from a branch and lands on the water in front of you.

As you watch this happen, start to become aware of your thoughts.

Each time a thought pops into your mind, imagine floating that thought out of your head and onto a leaf where you can watch it gently drifting past.

Don't try to make the stream go any faster or slower, or try to change the thought on the leaf. Just let it be.

Enjoy this process, and don't worry if you become distracted or it feels hard; just gently turn your attention back to noticing your thoughts, placing them on the leaves, and watching them float by.

CHAPTER 18

The Court of Law

The time has come to rethink your story of heartbreak through the lens of everything you now know.

The betrayal dropped a bomb on your life story, spreading outward from the epicenter of your life and destroying not only your own relationship narrative but the wider ones in which it was embedded. It's as if you were halfway through reading a great book, only to find the rest of the pages ripped out—and the bookshop you brought it from destroyed, along with your happy ending.

In your heart and mind you'd already written the whole story. Because our stories are so intimately connected with the people we love, when a significant relationship ends and, crucially here, not through our own choice, we struggle to reconcile what's happened with the story we always believed would play out. We were writing from a perspective that put our romantic relationship and our betrayal center stage. A perspective that allowed our heartbreak to define us. How about we choose something different now? How about we pick up those ripped-out pages, stick them back in, and carry on writing from a new perspective? You may not have chosen to be betrayed, but you can choose to be the author of what's next.

RUTH. I started my career as a lawyer, and practiced for a decade as a criminal attorney. I was terrified about my first speech to the jury and convinced I'd done an awful job, that my terror had been glaringly obvious to everyone in court and the jury members were bored. I entered the Bar robing rooms afterward armored up for criticism. The robing rooms are awash with backhanded banter, and I'm quite sure I gave as good as I got . . . "That was a forensic speech" (inference: *it was boring and long-winded*); "Lucky you, you've got such an easy case" (inference: *if you lose, you're a rubbish attorney*); "I love the way you jumped around with your questions" (inference: *your cross-examination was all over the place*).

But my opponent made a point of congratulating me af-

terward in the robing room. She was an older, seasoned attorney, and she told me how confident and convincing I'd
sounded, commenting that I'd structured the speech well,
starting with a powerful metaphor and finishing off with a
pithy summary. She also told me that the jury was hanging
on my every word. She may have been making it all up, of
course, to be kind, having spotted my nerves. And while I
continued to doubt her on the walk back home, I turned
what she'd said over and over in my mind. I respected and
admired her, so her comments were harder to dismiss, and
because the specifics of what she said were also plausible
(just about) and weren't compliments about how fabulous
I looked in my wig and gown, I chose to accept her offering
as another valid perspective on what had just happened.

She had given me something unexpected—a truthful
compliment. I hadn't been stung. I held what she'd said
close to my chest and reminded myself of that "jury hanging on my every word" comment whenever I was feeling
nervous and every time before giving a speech. It never
failed to give me a boost.

Have you ever had the experience of someone you respect recounting an experience in which you were the
main event, but completely differently to your recollec-

tion of it? Perhaps they emphasized a strength you hadn't paid attention to or a thoughtful response you didn't remember making, a power you hadn't valued?

This can go the other way too. Negative feedback you didn't see coming can feel like a slap in the face. The dentist once told me at a routine checkup that I had receding gums and promptly sent a referral letter to a periodontist for gum graft surgery. Having never noticed my receding gums before he did, it was all I could see afterward whenever I looked in the mirror. As it turns out, I reflected on what the dentist said and had the receding gums treated, and now I have teeth I'd never even realized I wanted.

Do share the love by telling someone how you see them and helping them change their narrative of themselves, like that lovely attorney did for me. It can have a huge impact on their day, sometimes their whole life.

There are perspectives about you too that haven't even occurred to you yet. And there will be things other people see in you that can help shift how you see yourself, even when it might sound less than full of praise.

There are caveats to this. Not everyone can be trusted in their commentary. Be careful who you pay attention to and whose comments you take on board. A good question to ask yourself might be: Does the person have any Dark Triad traits? Grant me the serenity to accept and the wisdom to spot Dark Triads—and always reject them out of hand! If their comments make you feel dismissed or helpless and desperate in any way, case dismissed. We all hurt each other sometimes and say regrettable things—because we are human. But it shouldn't routinely be the case. People you can trust will make you feel better or hopeful, even when what they have to say is challenging or critical.

And you still get to choose what comments to take on board. Always.

Another valuable lesson I learned at the Bar was how much more power story has over facts. Whether defending or prosecuting a case, both sides receive identical witness statements, police reports, telephone transcripts, forensic evidence, and photographs. Whichever side had instructed me, my job was to weave a story from that same bundle of evidence, a story which, by the end of the case—if I'd done a good enough job—would bear no resemblance whatsoever to my opponent's.

My task was to rework the facts and material in such a way as to make a defendant *appear* innocent or guilty in the eyes of the jury. Take a robbery case, for example.

The prosecution relied on the facts that a mobile phone had been stolen and a knife drawn, and that my client had been identified by the victim. The question I had to ask myself, representing the defendant, was: How can I present the facts of the knife and the phone and my client having been identified to tell a different story, a story aligned with my client's case, a story powerful enough to persuade a jury to acquit them? What was the defendant doing with this alleged knife? Indeed, was there a knife at all, or was it in fact a stainless steel ruler? Wasn't it awfully dark at the time? How can you be sure it was them? Were they even there at all? Perhaps it was someone else? There was no phone; you are mistaken. You have a grudge against them and have made it all up. That kind of thing.

The key skill was always to try to use what had happened (the facts) to tell the story in a new and surprising way that had perhaps not occurred to anyone yet. And it was clear that at the Bar, as in life, a lack of facts had little bearing on how compelling a narrative you could weave. Indeed, if both attorneys are any good, the jury often has the unenviable task of having to choose between two utterly different but equally compelling stories: one resulting in prison for the defendant, and the other, freedom.

*   *   *

Now for some fun...

You get to be the attorney for both sides. For and against. Pen and paper at the ready, please. Two columns. Write down the facts in defense of the fledgling belief in the first column. And only the facts (no conjecture, opinion, or assumption). In the second column, list all the facts against it. Only the facts, remember.

Let's hear from Nadia: Nadia's fledgling belief is that she is stupid. The facts in support of it are that she got the name of a bone wrong when she was six years old. The facts against it are that she got straight As at school, holds a degree in sociology, and heads up a team at work.

Everything she had been telling herself in support of the fledgling belief was the story she had weaved on the back of it: everyone else is smarter than me; I never know the answers, so I have to ask all the questions; my fiancée is smarter than me; my dad is smarter than me. She was constantly comparing herself to others and finding herself falling short.

Now it's your turn. Do the facts add up to the story you've been telling yourself? Put yourself in the position of judge and jury. Who wins?

In our experience, a fledgling belief gets calcified by the story woven around it and has little to do with facts. Once you can divorce the facts from the story, what becomes clearer is that your fledgling belief was one of your earliest stories, one of the core narratives, and so it's a sticky one, a very sticky one. But... the evidence you find to challenge it is in fact the seed of a new story. So keep at it, keep gathering the evidence for the new belief, keep weaving that new story, until it's as sticky as its predecessor. Sorry, what predecessor?

*   *   *

Deconstructing your own story in a court of law puts you back in charge of the narrative. Seeing yourself in your story from multiple different perspectives can help broaden and expand your sense of yourself, which brings other possible storylines into view. Your ability to rescript difficult material is a powerful weapon in your defense against the heartbreak.

Long after you've finished reading this book, you can revisit the idea of being a criminal attorney, rescript the case, and convict whatever sticky thought comes your way.

As you move forward, tuning in to your new narrative is key. For now, think of your fledgling belief and take a few minutes to write down any other beliefs about yourself that you may have formed around that time, within the context of your early nest. Now do the same for your flying belief, adding any other ones that occur to you about yourself. Now think of these two different accounts as two different radio stations. Give your fledgling beliefs station a name—for example, Limiting FM or Get Back in Your Box FM. This is the prosecutor's voice, always finding fault with you and damming you. Now give the flying station a name, something uplifting like Epic FM. Think of this station as your defense advocate and tune in to it whenever you feel that fledgling belief and strategy coming back into play. This is the most important frequency to tune in to. It is your wise adult empathetic mind, so turn up the volume when you get there.

Practice noticing when you are tuned in to each channel and the difference in your experience when listening to each one.

* * *

With your wise and empathetic adult mind at the helm, and the volume up high on Epic FM, it's time to write another story.

You don't have to restrict yourself to the heartbreak story, unless you'd like to. Once again, length, style, and tone are entirely up to you. You have a voice that is uniquely your own, which is infinitely more powerful than any other. What other people think has no place here. There is no right or wrong or better or worse way to do this because only you can tell your story.

We'd like you to frame it around the following questions. When considering these questions, reflect on all the insights you've gained about yourself, your heartbreaker, your attachment patterns, bonding blueprints, the dynamics of your early nest and your new perspectives. Keep your GPS to hand and radically accept everything!

What have you been through?

How have you coped?

What strategies have you used to keep yourself safe until now?

How are you going to move forward?

CHAPTER 19

Scene V

Once Upon a Time

Cozy den. Night.

In the den, the fire is roaring and all the women are
seated. There is a connectedness within the group and
the atmosphere is buoyant. Each of the women look
different; furrowed brows appear relaxed, smiles have
widened and deepened, eyes are twinkling; there is an
aliveness to them and they comment among themselves
on how fabulous they all look. ALICE tells them
it's a thing-the Heartbreak Hotel Botox Effect-and
everybody laughs. IRENE, with one arm draped across
the back of the sofa, says she feels as though her
whole brain has been Botoxed. ROBYN appears focused
and refreshed. ESHE is smiling and at ease, both
hands resting in her lap. LIN and NADIA occupy
their seats with a commanding presence, fully owning
their space. ALICE and RUTH turn toward LIN.

LIN: Okay, here goes. On his way to pick me up
         from gymnastics, my father died in a car
         crash. [*Deep breath, coughing fit.*] My
         mother was left to look after the whole
         family, and I, as the eldest, took on extra
         responsibilities because she was so busy.
         Although she put a brave face on it, I knew
         how sad she was. When her brother started
         coming over to help out, it cheered her up,
         it cheered us all up. But then he started to
         want to be alone with me, and that's when
         the rough-and-tumble became touching and
         stroking. I didn't tell anyone because I
         thought it was my fault. I thought it was

a punishment for killing my dad, because
if it wasn't for my gymnastics class, he'd
still be alive. I was confused, and because
I loved my uncle, and I loved my mother and
they loved each other and it seemed to make
him happy, which made her happy, I never
said a word. But I think she knew—how could
she not? And that made me think it must be
okay. But it wasn't. All these years I've
blamed my mother and in my head I've had
her in the dock over and over again [*Tears
rolling down her face.*] and convicted her
many times. Maybe when I grew up and left
home, I needed it to be her fault to make
sense of how I'd allowed it to happen, and
to cope with the fact that it had happened.
I don't know . . . But what I do know now
is that it was not my fault.

[*Pause.*]

And it was not my mother's fault either. It was my
uncle's fault.

[*Pause.*]

How have I coped? I coped by working hard and
winning prizes to ward off the feeling that I was
worth nothing. But no matter how well I did or

how many times I won a medal or a prize, I never
felt good enough. Nothing was ever enough to take
away the empty and worthless feeling that I had
as a child. And nobody cared anyway. I've been
running and running, yet somehow always ending up
in the same place, exhausting myself in the process.
And it's only now that I'm learning how to cope
differently, that I've started to think I might
be worth something after all. I am going to start
taking better care of myself, just like I do for
others . . . and leave those prizes behind.

[*Pause.*]

I was led straight into the arms of Dick Dust
because he had won even more prizes than me, which
I thought meant he must be a good person. He
was ambitious and gorgeous and came from a good
family that mine approved of. I was flattered by
all the attention and overlooked many red flags.
I met him after he gave a talk at the hospital
about anesthesia. I remember that same evening a
student nurse telling me that he was a cad, but
I completely dismissed her and instead let myself
become mesmerized by him. When he pulled my hair one
night at a friend's engagement party and the next
day laughed it off as a joke, I believed him, even
though my intuition told me it was wrong. He was
jealous and prone to violent outbursts, and it was

as unacceptable then as it is now-I just didn't see
it at the time. There were lots of incidents like
that, but I was so attracted to him, and believed
so strongly that we were "meant to be," with all
those things we had in common and my family's
enthusiasm, I was unable to see him for who he is.
Because of everything I have learned here, this is
how I am going to move forward:

[*Pause.*]

I will never fall for this sort of man again.
Until I came here, I thought there was something
wrong with me; I was good at my job but terrible
in relationships-maybe even that because I was
good at being a radiologist and so happy to be a
doctor, that there was a sort of justice to being
unlucky in love. Because you can't have everything,
can you? On some level, I believed that I deserved
nothing more than what I got from Dick Dust-crumbs
of love and affection I begged for at his feet like
a starving dog. I have no experience of what safety
looks like in a partner, but I'm determined to find
out. I might create a spreadsheet or-who knows-
develop an app or, at the very least, get potential
partners to answer a questionnaire. Maybe Nadia
can help me with that. [LIN *winks at* NADIA; ALL
smile.] Actually, there is a lovely man I know from
medical school who now works in pediatrics . . .

he might not dazzle like Dick Dust, but maybe he's
the safety I've been looking for. But first of all,
I've got to get Dick Dust out of the condo. [ALL
clap.] Before this retreat, I'd have married him if
he'd asked me to. Now I see I've dodged a bullet.
[ALL *cheer and laugh.*]

[*Pause.*]

All this time I've made excuses for him, even
enabled his behavior through my silence and
submission, and all the while blamed myself, and
my mother, when it is my uncle who is the one who
should be in the dock, and Dick Dust alongside him.
My mother may not be perfect, but I know that she
has her own demons to deal with and generations
of expectations on her tiny shoulders too. Maybe
she can come to the Heartbreak Hotel for the next
retreat; everybody in my family should come and
do this! Staying silent about all the things Dick
Dust has done and the things my uncle did has
created a lot of shame. I've learned that the only
way to make this better is by speaking it out loud.
Talking about what happened then, and what is
happening to me now, is how I will reclaim power
over my future and banish the shame. I've learned
from Robyn that doing one brave thing creates a
ripple, and if we all stand up together in this way
and call it out, we can make some serious waves—and
I've enough on Dick Dust to generate a tsunami.

[*Pause.*]

When I get back home, I'm going to make two phone
calls. The first to my mother. The second to the
police. None of it was my fault, and I am not
going to waste another minute of this precious life
living as though it was. [*Smiles through tears;*
ALL *applaud.*]

IRENE: I've been ever so careful for so long now.
Careful was how I ended up living in the
same town I grew up in. Careful was how I
married Stan-a man I was not even sexually
attracted to. But he was the safe choice.
Well, I thought he was, but now I see I
was living in his shadow and the shadow he
cast was long. He was careful too. Careful
with me. Careful with money. Careful with
his feelings. I don't want to do him down
because he was a good man; he never got
drunk, he never hit me, but . . . he liked
me in my place, and he didn't like it when
I stepped out of it or stood up for myself,
and you know what, he did whatever he
wanted, and went wherever he wanted and was
only able to build his business because of
me. And that's the truth. I'm thinking this
should have all gone in my first story,
but I guess I'm only being really honest
with myself now. I've had a good life,

never wanted for anything, so I thought
his behavior was a small price to pay. But
now I see maybe it was a bit more expensive
after all. I don't know. We were happy in
our own way, but I understood happiness as
being careful and safe. Careful was how I
was as a mother, and careful didn't keep my
sons close to me or to their sister. Far
from it. They now live on opposite sides
of the world. Maybe my being careful drove
them away because they felt suffocated. Who
knows. Careful didn't stop me from being
betrayed either. Being careful did not keep
me safe and it did not protect me from
pain.

[*Pause.*]

Now that I know how to turn down the volume on
the old familiar radio station and tune in to a
new, much kinder, wiser one—which, by the way, is
not at all careful and lives on a diet of radical
acceptance—I see it very differently and can tell my
story in a new way . . .

[*Pause.*]

Once upon a time there was a little girl who helped
her mummy with her baby brother and was always

cheerful. She loved climbing trees and running
free and had a daring spirit. Her daddy was
often away and this made her mummy sad, but the
little girl kept thinking, *If I try hard enough,
I can cheer Mummy up and she will be happy and
everything will be okay.* And nothing made the
little girl happier than making her mother laugh.
Because she was such a good little girl, her
mummy gave her bigger jobs: taking the baby to
the park and making meals. The little girl loved
this because she liked to pretend she was a mummy
too and that her little brother was her own baby.
It was all part of the adventure. The little girl
wanted to cheer her mummy up on her birthday.
She couldn't get her out of bed, and the little
girl didn't understand that it was because she
was depressed and that it had nothing to do with
her. Then the little girl nearly killed her baby
brother with the boiling water from the kettle,
and she decided that she was a bad girl after
all. The little girl decided that the world was a
dangerous place and that everything was scary and
that it was better to be careful and then everyone
would be safe.

[*Pause.*]

It didn't matter that she missed climbing trees and
paddling in the stream because the more careful she

was, the fewer things went wrong. Being careful was
working; her baby brother didn't get hurt again-
even though his scarred face reminded the little
girl each day how close he had come to death-
and her mummy did start talking to her again,
eventually. The little girl missed her adventuring,
but it seemed worth it to keep everyone safe, and so
she gave up on her dream of becoming an explorer.
The little girl decided a life of adventure was a
very bad idea, as accidents do happen, and to stop
bad things from happening you have to be very, very
careful.

[*Pause.*]

The little girl grew up and didn't stray far from
home. She married the surest, safest boy from her
school. As a big girl, she tried very hard never
to argue with her husband, but to swallow all
his put-downs and always be careful-even with her
feelings, and especially with her temper. She was so
good at being careful that she forgot she even had
one. She forgot she had feelings at all. When her
husband died, she was careful in her grief, careful
not to let it show in case she upset her grown-up
children. She was careful and she was lonely. And
because she didn't believe in herself and hadn't
had much of a sex life, when Lucifer came along,

she was flattered by all the attention and let her
guard down. Because she loved him, she would have
done anything for him, so she gave him money for
his brother. She was furious when she found out
she'd been played, because she had been so careful
and couldn't understand that such a bad thing had
happened to such a careful person . . . until she
went back in time and met up with the young girl
she once was, standing next to her burning brother
with the kettle at his feet, and took hold of her
little hand and told her that it was not her fault-
that none of it was her fault. [*Voice shaky, tears
welling.*]

[*Pause.*]

The truth is this insight has only been made
possible because of my betrayal. He can have the
money. I have my freedom now. I might be too old
to climb trees, but then again . . . [*Whoops from
ALL.*]

[*Pause.*]

The good thing about having been so careful is that
Stan and I were careful with money too, and he made
quite a bit of it. So even though Lucifer stole a
lot, I've no mortgage to pay and more than enough

to live off-if I'm careful . . . only joking! I'm
never using that word again. Instead of a swear
jar, I'm going to have a "careful" jar, and if
I ever do anything "careful," or use the word at
all, I'll put a pound into that jar and use all
the money to do something seriously bloody un-
careful. I'm done with it. I've always been drawn
to India, but never allowed myself to follow up
on it, because of course, there's nothing careful
about traveling to the Himalayas to go trekking.
[*Cheering.*] My friend Claire might even fancy
joining me, and I'm going to ask her as soon as I
get home. [NADIA *wolf-whistles.*]

[*Pause.*]

I'm going on an adventure. I gave up on all that
because of an accident that had nothing to do with
me. So . . . it's first stop India, and then on to
my grandchildren in Australia, where I'm going to
take them to do something daring and wild. My sons
won't recognize me. I've not got it all planned out
either, because I trust now that it's all going to
be okay, that I'm going to be okay. We're all going
to be okay. [ALL *clap;* ALICE *looks to* NADIA *and
nods.*]

NADIA: Looking back, I know I was lucky to
        have such good parents and no siblings,

especially after hearing what you lot had
to put up with-no offense. [*Wry smile.*]
But I also think that because they are good
people and so accepting about my sexuality,
I glossed over the fact that there was other
stuff going on that restricted me from
developing fully. I never would have thought
that asking lots of questions could be a
problem, but I see now that I've worn my
questions like a shield to defend against
anyone getting to really know me and
finding out that I'm stupid. And I wasn't
always tuned in to the answers, which often
rebounded off me because it wasn't curiosity
driving them, but fear. I asked questions
so I would stay hidden and I now see that
this is why I have struggled to make close
connections. People liked me because my
questions made them feel special, and Frosty
was attracted to me because I seemed so
interested in everything she said and did.
And I think it made her feel important,
which I guess was her stuff, having come
from a chaotic home where she was largely
ignored. My questions gave her what she
didn't get growing up-a feeling of being
valued. But once the honeymoon period wore
off, she stopped being interested in me, and
neither of us could recapture that initial

chemistry. We were a typical Lone and Close
Ranger pairing. After the intensity wore
off, she started retreating whenever I came
near, and the more I tried to find her and
draw her back to me, the farther away she
went. As time marched on, we went off-key
and couldn't get back in tune no matter how
hard we tried.

[*Pause.*]

I don't feel good about what happened. I am still
heartbroken, and I don't want to forgive her
for what she did-and I'm glad you never asked
me to, because I don't and I won't. But what I
can do is accept my part in the breakdown of our
relationship. Because of my difficulties with
communicating freely and openly, and my fear of
being seen as stupid, and therefore rejected, I
couldn't really cope when things started to go
wrong. I became desperate for her attention rather
than accepting that maybe she just needed some
space. I'm grateful I got clear about that because
I know exactly what's needed now to move forward
and how to create a good relationship with a
future wife. My values will steer me on the right
course: Industry is going to propel me forward in
my career, which has stagnated because I have been
afraid. Passion is what's going to inspire me; by

letting it lead me, I'll get to know what really
makes me tick. Next is courage-to go for things,
even though I might be afraid. And my fourth value
is to manifest the spirit of abundance because I
want to live a life that's full to the brim.

[*Pause.*]

I was a lonely little girl and I've never admitted
that to myself or my family. I spent a lot of time
reading and playing on my own in my bedroom. That
was my safe place, my happy place. And it still
can be my happy place, so long as I'm also able
to be with others in a real and honest way and
not hide myself from everyone. I have another voice
that's not always quiet and questioning, which has
been hidden behind the curtain of long-ago beliefs
created by a six-year-old who didn't ever again
want to be humiliated by not knowing the answer.
This other voice is clear and sure of itself, if a
little out of practice. So . . . that's me. I am
capable and smart and I have a voice.

ALICE: You are and you do, Nadia. Now Robyn, we're
        so glad you're still here and didn't leave
        yesterday. Are you ready?

ROBYN: Yes, I am. And thank you, Alice and Ruth,
        for not kicking me out. My God, yesterday

feels like a thousand years ago now. I'm so
glad I stayed. Now that I have my values
GPS steering me right, I will celebrate
connection in all my relationships. Cherish
my physical and mental health. Find joy in
the everyday. Live a life of integrity and
honor my word. Those are my values and I
love them all!

[*Pause.*]

The biggest one for me is connection. I want to
reconnect with my daughters. I now see their low
opinion of me is a result of my addiction. But the
addiction is not who I am; it is how I have coped.
I'm going to have compassion for myself and not
beat myself up about it any longer. I will ask for
their forgiveness, and I will forgive myself. I
will own up to what's been going on for me, rejoin
Alcoholics Anonymous (AA), and take each day as
it comes. This time it will be different because I
have you good women to keep me straight and I have
all this knowledge and wisdom that has come from
doing this work. When I wake up with the jitters at
3 a.m., Lin will be in the middle of the afternoon
and might be on a break and Eshe will be making the
little one's breakfast. What I mean is, whatever
state we are in at whatever time of day or night,
all of us are only ever one text message away from

each other. That is such a wonderful thought, isn't
it? What a gift.

[*Pause.*]

I failed with AA before because my fledgling beliefs
were that everything's unfair, everyone hates me,
I'm ridiculous, and my feelings are irrelevant.
To cope with all this, I shut myself away from
everybody, I shut myself down. I thought in doing
this I wouldn't be blamed or hurt. But instead,
when I cut off from everybody, I got blamed anyway
and I hurt myself and my daughters through my
drinking. You heard it here first.

As you know, my husband and I built a home together
in Southwest France to retire to. But if I'm being
honest, I was only ever half there throughout the
marriage. The drinking started after our first
daughter. I had postnatal depression and was
self-medicating-although that is no excuse. I was
afraid to ask for help. I always thought I was
independent, but I was actually codependent and my
partner in crime was the alcohol. My girls deserve
better than that, and I deserve better too. I know
that I grew up in a dodgy nest, but I'm not going
to let that define me anymore. Yes, my brother was
a bully, but he had a hard time too. I can see that
now.

[*Pause.*]

As for Voldemort, the sad truth is that, yes,
he has left me for a more soulful love. God,
his midlife crisis is such a cliché. But I was
disconnected a lot of the time, and because of that
I wasn't able to be intimate with him. All his
requests for a cuddle were met with me running for
the hills, often with a bottle of vodka in my back
pocket. He has been horrible to me, and I don't
excuse him any of his behavior. To leave me so soon
after my diagnosis is callous and cruel. However,
I do feel that my greatest betrayal has come from
me-against myself. And bringing that into the light
is what's going to save me. Not reconciling with an
arsehole who left me when I needed him most. I want
to end my story by saying something to Lin. [ROBYN
turns toward LIN, *who puts her hand on her heart
and smiles.*]

[*Pause.*]

I came back because of you. When you told us about
your uncle, I remembered my own abuse, something
that I'd buried so deep and for so long, I had
almost forgotten it happened. I'd inebriated
myself against it rising up to the surface. I was
terrified of the feelings that came with the awful
memories, so I got in my car and left. But then I

thought of you and I didn't want you to feel shame in having bravely shared what had happened to you or to think I couldn't handle hearing it-and so I came back. Because of all of you here, when I got back to my room, I didn't have a drink. [*Reaches into her bag, pulls out unopened gin bottle, and places it on the table, hands shaking.*]

Because of you, I told my story too. Thank you, Lin, for the gift of you, for the gift of sharing your story. Your vulnerability became my courage.

[LIN *stands, goes to* ROBYN *for a big hug; when everyone is settled again,* ALICE *turns to* ESHE.]

ESHE: Robyn, I've got so much from you this weekend. Both my parents drank; they worked long hours in grueling jobs and I was left in charge a lot. Because of the drinking, they were often absent or angry for no reason, which is why I had to be so vigilant all the time and was too scared to ask them for help. I see now that my anxiety stemmed from my upbringing, which was busy and chaotic with everybody battling for Mum's attention.

[*Pause.*]

When Robyn talked about her daughters not trusting
her and blaming them, it really reminded me of my
own parents; it's exactly what they did-blamed me
for things going wrong, things that were their
responsibility, not mine. So thank you, Robyn,
for admitting to being an alcoholic so I could
realize my own parents were too. [*A nod between*
ESHE *and* ROBYN.] And I don't blame them, or anyone
else for that matter. My dad thought his anger
issues were nothing compared to his own father's,
who once broke his arm with a branch he'd snapped
off a tree. He told us this story to legitimize the
violence he used against us. He never used a stick
or a belt or a shoe; *we didn't know how easy we had
it,* he'd say . . . that sort of thing. God only
knows what his father's parents were like, but I'm
going to take a wild guess and say they probably
weren't the best, and not blame them either. Because
what's the point? My dad's drinking got worse after
Mum died, and he became more and more distant from
us and from himself. I see now this is an exact
mirror of my husband's behavior in our marriage
and that none of it is my fault.

[*Pause.*]

I was constantly fluffing up Ball Sack-that sounds
so wrong!

[*Giggles from* ALL.]

I did everything I could to please him, but it
was never going to be enough, which meant it could
never be right between us. He'll never be right for
anyone, because they won't satisfy him either. No
one can. I hate the phrase *sex addiction*-it sounds
like an excuse men invented for themselves to get
away with their sexual greed-but maybe there is
something to it. We were having sex the whole time
he was at it online and offline with these other
women. Even if we'd had sex twice a day, he'd have
still found time to betray me. Despite all this,
I can't remember ever feeling so free as I do right
now in this very moment.

[*Pause.*]

There wasn't much talk of feelings where I grew
up. Everybody was too busy trying to survive.
But my feelings have been there all along; even if
they never had a name or a time or a place to just
be, it didn't mean they weren't there. I tried to
get away from them because I lived in fear of them
controlling me. But I don't have to live like that
anymore. Just learning to let the feelings come,

knowing that they will pass, has been a revelation.
After this weekend, I am going to trust them more and
listen to what else my anger might be telling me.

[*Pause.*]

I am a Roller Ranger, but nothing is going to
overwhelm me. I know that now. If I notice myself
struggling against what's happening, I'll get out
my Chinese finger trap to remind myself how to let
go. So thank you for showing me the way, and for
being the green that I so badly needed. When I came
on this retreat, I thought that I still loved Ball
Sack and that I couldn't raise our children on my
own. I was hoping to find the strength to forgive
him and to allow him to come back to us. But now
I see how far away from myself I had traveled.
In this journey alongside all you amazing women
I have finally arrived-not where I imagined, but
back home. Back home with myself. My heart may
have been broken, but I'm no longer ruminating on
why he was so sweet on me once and how it all went
sour. Released from the chains of self-blame, I
can feel my spirit growing strong again. I will
rise from the ashes of my loss, and my children
will rise with me. Because if I am not afraid to
stride out on my own and build something new, they
won't be afraid to follow. I know who I am now,

and maybe that's all any of us ever really need to
know. My name is Eshe, and I matter.

ALICE: Reader, are you ready to share your story
with us?

CHAPTER 20

Daring to Choose

Forest fires burn away undergrowth that prevents sunlight reaching the forest floor—sunlight that enables new plants to grow on the ashes of the old. Fire is the disruptor that drives growth, giving both plant and animal species new opportunities to grow strong. It turns out that even something as devastating as a forest fire makes a vital contribution to the health of the forest.

Your heartbreak is that forest fire, and in the ashes of your loss seeds of new growth have taken root. To grow that precious seed of hope within you, accept that the fire has happened. Day after day, hour after hour, minute after minute, choose to accept—radically—that your heart has been broken. It was not your choice, and you can't change that it happened, but you do have choices now. And it is these choices that can turn the scorched landscape of your soul into the birthplace of your hope.

Which scenarios and choices are you struggling with at the moment? We'd invite you to write them down and place them on a continuum, with those you have the least control over at one end and those you have the most control over at the other. Here are some examples from your fellow guests.

> They never pick up the kids on time.
>
> Are they going to make me move out of the house?
>
> Will they come back to me?
>
> Am I going to file for divorce?
>
> Do they still love me?

If any of your scenarios fall toward the "no control" end of the continuum, let go of the rope. And for those scenarios and choices that you *can* do something about, write down some different courses of action you could take. Once you have two or three feasible options, we'd invite you to choose the one most aligned with your values and take the first step toward making it happen.

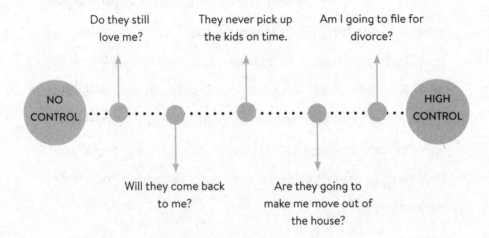

There is another choice that frames everything that is happening around you: the meaning that you give it. From the moment we are born, our task is to make meaning from our experience against a backdrop of uncertainty that there is any meaning at all. We imbue our experience with significance so that we can anchor ourselves and create a degree of coherence and predictability in our lives. *Why are we here?* is perhaps the biggest existential question of all, and no one has yet found a universally satisfactory answer. For some, we are fulfilling the will of God; for others we are slowly making our way along the evolutionary chain. Without any universal truth, we are responsible for creating our own sense of meaning throughout our lives. And meaning is not just a response to our experience; meaning *creates* our experience. Remember the perspective picture, where you could see both the duck and the rabbit? This is your mind's capacity to attribute different meanings to the same image, reflected in the perspective you choose to adopt.

If your heartbreaker was unfaithful, here are some meaning choices you could make:

They were a sex addict.

They were a narcissist who sought only their own pleasure.

I'm unlovable.

They left because I'm not attractive enough.

The world is an unfair place; many wonderful women get betrayed.

It shouldn't have happened; my life is over.

And it's not just for the big stuff: we make meaning choices about our everyday difficulties too. Let's say your heartbreaker isn't returning your calls. You could choose to attach any one of these different meanings to that fact (and feel free to add your own):

They didn't get the message.

I am ugly/fat/stupid.

They hate me.

They are punishing me.

I am irrelevant.

They are in bed with their lover.

I am unlovable.

They are a narcissistic twat.

The meaning you make affects the feelings you have about what happened. And the meaning is yours to choose. Always.

CHAPTER 21

A Mighty Wind

The smallest action you take now can have great significance on your life in ways you might never imagine.
Chaos theory teaches us that the outcome of any process
is sensitive to its starting point but may bear no resemblance to it: a butterfly flaps its wings in Brazil and the tiny
amount of air pressure it exerts causes a typhoon in Texas.

This is what's possible for you—and for all women. What
you do next counts. What we all do next counts—in all
kinds of unforeseen ways. You may not see a clear path-
way forward just yet. Sometimes you will find yourself
in a dense fog and all you can see is what's right in front
of you—and that's okay, because all you ever need is your
next move. And if you lead from your flying belief, you're

heading toward hope; if you lead with compassion and courage, you're heading toward confidence; if you lead with your values, you are heading toward purpose and joy. You have dared to explore who you are, you have dared to connect to your deepest vulnerabilities, and you have dared to choose to let go. Knowledge may be power, but insight is alchemy.

Keep that photo of your younger self near. Look after her, remember her dreams, and tend to her needs. Sweep away any shameful beliefs she held; they weren't meant for her and they are not meant for you. You deserve kindness and respect and love, and so does she.

Refusing to be diminished by those around you is an act of resistance—you are not less than anyone else and you are more than you ever imagined.

You don't need to do this alone. When women connect with one another in deep empathy and sit in silence as each speaks her truth, this act of unity and love sends out a powerful message—that we all stand together. This is how we build each other up. When you are in pain, remember others are too. Connect with them. Coming together and sharing our vulnerability is how we both join the dots of our experience and join hands with each other. Find your people. It is your community that will carry you. As you move forward, take what you have learned, advocate for it–amplify it–because it is relevant to everyone. Link up with others and lean out. Love wisely, stand up for each other, and share your stories.

Our hope for you is that you choose to think and act in ways that build you up. That you take responsibility only for what you can control. That you take the definitions others give you with a pinch of salt if they make you feel any less of a woman. That you act in service to your values. That you take the time you need–less than you imagine, but more than you will want to give. That you let go of the rope, or don't pick it up at all. That you keep yourself cozy, have a good laugh when you can, and always take that nap.

You have what you need now. So keep making your next move, and before you know it, you'll be somewhere you never thought you'd be. It's not for us to know where that is. But we do know that you have many possibilities, and it is within these that your hope lies.

Imagine this...

All the strength and all the vulnerability of all the women all over the world circulating like starlings in the sky, in perfect unison and beautiful formation. Think of the air pressure it would create; nothing would ever be the same again. The power generated would raise from the ground all those on their knees and show them how much they matter, just as you do.

Spread your wings ... a mighty wind is coming.

Epilogue

Nadia was promoted to head of HR for a global organization and relocated to New York, where she has set up home with her gorgeous kitten, Cookie. She is enjoying answering more questions than she's asking.

Irene's latest update on the WhatsApp group was a photo she posted of herself white water rafting down the Zambezi.

Lin is dating the pediatrician. She doesn't know it yet, but tonight when he takes her for a birthday supper, he's going to propose. In case you are worried about his attachment pedigree, he is a Safe Harbor. Her mother is going to be their best woman.

Eshe is studying for a PhD alongside her senior lectureship. On weekends, she volunteers at the domestic violence shelter with her eldest daughter.

Robyn's unmentionable is living in France with the mosaic tile man he met in Santorini. She is reconnecting with her daughters and she still hasn't had a drink.

As for you . . . do let us know.

Acknowledgments

Special thanks...

To our number one champion and a stellar agent, Chandler Crawford, and the team at Transatlantic Literary Agency for launching our book into the world.

To our forensic and sensitive editors on both sides of the pond—Judith Curr, Elizabeth Mitchell, and Louise McKeever—and to the phenomenon that is Lisa Milton, for stewarding us through the entire process and for being, well, one of the most epic women to walk the earth.

Thanks to the powerhouse that is Cathryn Summerhayes, our brilliant agent, and everyone involved at Curtis Brown.

To assistant editor Ghjulia Romiti, production editor Crissie Johnson Molina, copyeditor Tanya Fox, and proofreader Stephanie Baker for doing such an eagle-eyed job of polishing the manuscript. To Leah Carlson-Stanisic for the interior design and to Stephen Brayda for the cover.

To our friends and champions from far and wide, for the listening and advising and endless support and cheer-leading.

To our families—in particular, Jean-Paul, Sonny, Isla, Olly, Rufus, and Sebastian—for facilitating the writing trips, never losing faith, and inspiring us in all manner of ways.

To each other for all the hard thinking and endless re-writes, for spurring each other on when we didn't think we had anything left in the tank, and for still making each other laugh, even when another little darling was up for the chop.

To all our women from all around the world who have connected with us at the Heartbreak Hotel and who have come on retreat. You're the reason we're all here. Keep on shining so others can too.

Notes

Introduction

1. Infidelity is an emotional or physical act constituting a break of trust.

2. Kristina Coop Gordon, Donald H. Baucom, and Douglas K. Snyder, "An Integrative Intervention for Promoting Recovery from Extramarital Affairs," *Journal of Marital and Family Therapy* 30, no. 2 (April 2004): 213–31, https://doi .org/10.1111/j.1752-0606.2004.tb01235.x.

3. Michael Linden, "Posttraumatic Embitterment Disorder," *Psychotherapy and Psychosomatics* 72, no. 4 (July–August 2003): 195–202, https://doi.org/10.1159/000070783.

4. N. Padmavathi, T. S. Sunitha, and G. Jothimani, "Post Infidelity Stress Disorder," *Indian Journal of Psychiatric Nursing* 5, no. 1 (2013): 56–59, https://doi.org/10.4103/2231-1505.261777.

5. Victoria Williamson, Dominic Murphy, Andrea Phelps, David Forbes, and Neil Greenberg, "Moral Injury: The Effect on Mental Health and Implications for Treatment," *The Lancet Psychiatry* 8, no. 6 (2021): 453–55.

6. Timothy R. Levine, *Duped: Truth-Default Theory and the Social Science of Lying and Deception* (Tuscaloosa: Univ. Alabama Press, 2020).

7. Rowena Pagdin, Paul M. Salkovskis, Falguni Nathwani, Megan Wilkinson-Tough, and Emma Warnock-Parkes, "'I Was Treated like Dirt': Evaluating Links between Betrayal and Mental Contamination in Clinical Samples," *Behavioural and Cognitive Psychotherapy* 49, no. 1 (2021): 21–34, https://doi.org/10.1017/S1352465820000387.

8. Brian D. Earp, Olga A. Wudarczyk, Bennett Foddy, and Julian Savulescu, "Addicted to Love: What Is Love Addiction and When Should It Be Treated?," *Philosophy, Psychiatry, & Psychology* 24, no. 1 (March 2017): 77–92, https://doi.org/10.1353/ppp.2017.0011.

9. Dean Takahashi, "Ashley Madison: Affairs in the Time of Coronavirus," *Venture Beat*, March 28, 2020, https://venturebeat.com/2020/03/28/ashley-madison-affairs-in-the-time-of-coronavirus/.

10. Sebastian, "Ashley Madison User, Growth and Cheating Statistics (2022)," RelationshipAdvice.co, last modified August 11, 2023, https://relationshipsadvice.co/ashley-madison-statistics/.

11. Kristina Coop Gordon and Erica A. Mitchell, "Infidelity in the Time of COVID-19," *Family Process* 59, no. 3 (September 2020): 956–66, https://doi.org/10.1111/famp.12576.

12. Benjamin Warach and Lawrence Josephs, "The Aftershocks of Infidelity: A Review of Infidelity-Based Attachment Trauma," *Sexual and Relationship Therapy* 36, no. 1 (2019): 68–90, https://doi.org/10.1080/14681994.2019.1577961.

13. Howard E. LeWine, "Broken-Heart Syndrome (Takotsubo Cardiomyopathy)," Harvard Health Publishing: Harvard Medical School, June 13, 2023, https://www.health.harvard.edu/heart-health/takotsubo-cardiomyopathy-broken-heart-syndrome.

14. Communications Team, "First Treatment for 'Broken Heart Syndrome' Trialled," University of Aberdeen, June 29, 2022, https://www.abdn.ac.uk/news/16140/.

15. Howard E. LeWine, "Broken-Heart Syndrome."

16. Sandeep M. Patel, Ramesh G. Chokka, Kavita Prasad, and Abhiram Prasad, "Distinctive Clinical Characteristics According to Age and Gender in Apical Ballooning Syndrome (Takotsubo/Stress Cardiomyopathy): An Analysis Focusing on Men and Young Women," *Journal of Cardiac Failure* 19, no. 5 (May 2013): 306–10, https://doi.org/10.1016/j.cardfail.2013.03.007.

17. Victoria L. Cammann, Konrad A. Szawan, Barbara E. Stähli, Ken Kato, et al., "Age-Related Variations in Takotsubo Syndrome," *Journal of the American College of Cardiology* 75, no. 16 (2020): 1869–77, https://doi.org/10.1016/j.jacc.2020.02.018.

18. Jieun Lee, Amy Wachholtz, and Keum-Hyeong Choi, "A Review of the Korean Cultural Syndrome Hwa-Byung: Suggestions for Theory and Intervention," *Asia Taepyongyang Sangdam Yongu* 4, no. 1 (January 2014): 49, https://doi.org/10.18401/2014.4.1.4.

19. Hyo-Weon Suh, Ki-Beom Lee, Sun-Yong Chung, Minjung Park, Bo-Hyoung Jang, and Jong Woo Kim, "How Suppressed Anger Can Become an Illness: A Qualitative Systematic Review of the Experiences and Perspectives of Hwabyung Patients in Korea," *Frontiers in Psychiatry* 12 (2021): 637029, https://doi.org/10.3389/fpsyt.2021.637029.

20. Sara Wallström, Kerstin Ulin, Sylvia Määttä, Elmir Omerovic, and Inger Ekman, "Impact of Long-Term Stress in Takotsubo Syndrome: Experience of Patients," *European Journal of Cardiovascular Nursing* 15, no. 7 (December 2016): 522–28, https://doi.org/10.1177/1474515115618568.

Chapter 2: Your Story

1. Stephen J. Lepore, Melanie A. Greenberg, Michelle Bruno, and Joshua M. Smyth, "Expressive Writing and Health: Self-Regulation of Emotion-Related Experience, Physiology, and Behavior," in *The Writing Cure: How Expressive Writing Promotes Health and Emotional Well-Being*, eds. Stephen J. Lepore and Joshua M. Smyth (Washington, DC: American Psychological Association, 2002), 99–117, https://doi.org/10.1037/10451-005.

2. Deborah Siegel-Acevedo, "Writing Can Help Us Heal from Trauma," *Harvard Business Review*, July 1, 2021, https://hbr.org/2021/07/writing-can-help-us-heal-from-trauma.

3. Joanne Frattaroli, "Experimental Disclosure and Its Moderators: A Meta-Analysis," *Psychological Bulletin* 132, no. 6 (2006): 823–65, https://doi.org/10.1037/0033-2909.132.6.823.

4. The Dropping Anchor metaphor is adapted from Russ Harris, *The Happiness Trap: How to Stop Struggling and Start Living* (Umhlanga Rocks, South Africa: Trumpeter Books, 2008).

Chapter 4: Rumination

1. Namiko Kamijo and Shintaro Yukawa, "The Role of Rumination and Negative Affect in Meaning Making Following Stressful Experiences in a Japanese Sample," *Frontiers in Psychology* 9 (November 2018): 2404, https://doi.org/10.3389/fpsyg.2018.02404.

2. Samantha M. Jones and Erin A. Heerey, "Co-Rumination in Social Networks," *Emerging Adulthood* 10, no. 6 (2022), 1345–60, https://doi.org/10.1177/21676968221111316.

3. Ashley Borders, "Consequences of Expressed Rumination," in
    Ruminations and Related Constructs: Causes, Consequences,
    and Treatment of Thinking Too Much (London: Academic Press,
    2020), 169–98, https://www.sciencedirect.com/science/article
    /pii/B9780128125458000061#s0060.

4. Thomas F. Denson, "The Multiple Systems Model of Angry
    Rumination," *Personality and Social Psychology Review* 17, no. 2
    (2013), 103–23, https://doi.org/10.1177/1088868312467086.

5. Denson, "Multiple Systems Model of Angry Rumination."

6. The Tiger Cub metaphor is adapted from Steven C. Hayes,
    Get Out of Your Mind and Into Your Life: The New Acceptance
    and Commitment Therapy (Oakland, CA: New Harbinger
    Publications, 2005).

7. The Chinese Finger Trap metaphor is adapted from Hayes, *Get*
    Out of Your Mind.

Chapter 5: Scene II

1. Adapted from Paul McKenna, *Instant Influence and Charisma:*
    Master the Art of Natural Charm and Ethical Persuasiveness
    (London: Bantam, 2015).

Chapter 6: Radical Acceptance

1. Jeffrey Brantley, Jeffrey C. Wood, and Matthew McKay, *The*
    Dialectical Behavior Therapy Skills Workbook (Oakland, CA:
    New Harbinger, 2007).

2. The Troll and the Hole metaphor is adapted from Steven C.
    Hayes, *Get Out of Your Mind and Into Your Life: The New*

Acceptance and Commitment Therapy (Oakland, CA: New Harbinger Publications, 2005).

Chapter 8: Bonding Blueprints

1. Kelly-Ann Allen, Margaret L. Kern, Christopher S. Rozek, Dennis M. McInerney, and George M. Slavich, "Belonging: A Review of Conceptual Issues, an Integrative Framework, and Directions for Future Research," *Australian Journal of Psychology* 73, no. 1 (2021): 87–102, https://doi.org/10.1080/00049530.2021.1883409.

2. Jill Sakai, "How Synaptic Pruning Shapes Neural Wiring during Development and, Possibly, in Disease," *PNAS* 17, no. 28 (July 14, 2020): 16096–99, https://doi.org/10.1073/pnas.2010281117.

3. Harry F. Harlow and Margaret Harlow, "Learning to Love," *American Scientist* 54, no. 3 (1966): 244–72, http://www.jstor.org/stable/27836477.

4. John Bowlby, *Attachment*, 2nd ed. (New York: Basic Books, 1982).

5. This term corresponds to the more commonly used *secure attachment style*.

6. This term corresponds to the more commonly used *avoidant attachment style*.

7. This term corresponds to the more commonly used *anxious attachment style*.

8. This term corresponds to the more commonly used *disorganized attachment style*.

9. Jeffry A. Simpson and W. Steven Rholes, "Adult Attachment, Stress, and Romantic Relationships," *Current Opinion in Psychology* 13 (February 2017): 19–24, https://doi.org/10.1016/j.copsyc.2016.04.006.

Chapter 9: The Dark Triad

1. Monica A. Koehn, Ceylan Okan, and Peter K. Jonason, "A Primer on the Dark Triad Traits," *Australian Journal of Psychology* 71, no. 1 (2019): 7–15, https://doi.org/10.1111/ajpy.12198.

2. Lawrence Josephs, "Fatal Attractions: The Dark Triad and Infidelity," in *The Dynamics of Infidelity: Applying Relationship Science to Psychotherapy Practice* (Washington, DC: American Psychological Association, 2018), 89–111, https://doi.org/10.1037/0000053-005.

3. Grant Hilary Brenner, "11 Ways People Try to Hide Their Infidelity: 5. Use Friends for Coverage," *Psychology Today*, January 9, 2022, https://www.psychologytoday.com/gb/blog/experimentations/202201/the-top-11-ways-people-try-hide-infidelity.

4. Timothy R. Levine, *Duped: Truth-Default Theory and the Social Science of Lying and Deception* (Tuscaloosa: Univ. of Alabama Press, 2020).

Chapter 13: Power and Shame

1. Joanne L. Bagshaw, *The Feminist Handbook* (Oakland, CA: New Harbinger, 2019).

Chapter 15: Emotional Regulation

1. Adapted from Paul Gilbert, *The Compassionate Mind* (London: Constable, 2010).

2. I. Jarero and L. Artigas, "The EMDR Integrative Group Treatment Protocol: EMDR Group Treatment for Early Intervention following Critical Incidents," *European Review of Applied Psychology* 62, no. 4 (October 2012): 219–22, https://doi.org/10.1016/j.erap.2012.04.004.

Chapter 16: The Compass

1. The Rickety Train metaphor is adapted from Jill A. Stoddard and Niloofar Afari, *The Big Book of ACT Metaphors: A Practitioner's Guide to Experiential Exercises and Metaphors in Acceptance and Commitment Therapy* (Oakland, CA: New Harbinger Publications, 2014).

Chapter 17: New Perspectives

1. The Floating Leaves metaphor is adapted from Jill A. Stoddard and Niloofar Afari, *The Big Book of ACT Metaphors: A Practitioner's Guide to Experiential Exercises and Metaphors in Acceptance and Commitment Therapy* (Oakland, CA: New Harbinger Publications, 2014).

Alice Haddon and **Ruth Field** have been friends for thirty years, sharing their stories and supporting each other through their many heartbreaks. Alice is a counseling psychologist with twenty-five years' experience in both public and private psychology services. She also works as an academic and lecturer at the City, University of London. Ruth is a coach and motivational self-help author with a master's degree in creative writing. She spent a decade working as a criminal attorney. Both women are passionate advocates for women's mental health. Alice is an associate fellow of the British Psychological Society and a Health and Care Professionals Council registered practitioner psychologist. Ruth is a member of the Criminal Bar Association, the Association for Coaching, and the International Society for Coaching Psychology.